W9-BZW-870

MEA ROMA

MARTIAL
(M. VALERIUS MARTIALIS)

MEA ROMA

TRANSLATED FROM LATIN BY

ART BECK

SHEARSMAN BOOKS

First published in the United Kingdom in 2018 by
Shearsman Books
50 Westons Hill Drive
Emersons Green
BRISTOL
BS16 7DF

Shearsman Books Ltd Registered Office
30–31 St. James Place, Mangotsfield, Bristol BS16 9JB
(this address not for correspondence)

www.shearsman.com

ISBN 978-1-84861-618-9

ACKNOWLEDGEMENTS
A number of these poems were included in essays
published in the following E-Journals:

'Blood on the Jumbotron – Martial's Arena Poems.'
The Critical Flame, May 2015.
'The Power of Three, Some Martial Triptychs.'
Your Impossible Voice, November 2015.
'Two Latin Poets.' *Journal of Poetics Research,* Issue 4, 2016.
'I Really Hate You Doctor Fell, But Love's Funny that Way'
Journal of Poetics Research, Issue 5, 2016
'Eros and Possession, Martial's Diadumenus Epigrams,'
Queen Mob's Teahouse, January 2017
'This Powerful Rhyme,' *Journal of Poetics Research,* Issue 7, 2017
'A Poem that Sleeps with the Fishes', *Journal of Poetics Research,* Issue 8, 2018'

21 of the poems were published in the chapbook,
Epigrams, Magra Books, Bagnone, Italy/Los Angeles, May 2016.

CONTENTS

MEA ROMA

I. WHY?

Anyone hoping to lure a reader into yet another new version of an old chestnut should be expected to address that simple question. Martial, particularly warrants this kind of prefatory discussion because he's left us over 1,500 extant poems. There are two complete Loeb, prose versions, but the size of the canon pretty well precludes a complete verse attempt by any one poet. So selection choice becomes in itself an aesthetic of translation.

This selection began a few years ago when I decided to try translating Martial's *Liber Spectaculorum*. I, initially, thought that 37-poem sequence set in the Roman Colosseum might make an interesting chapbook-sized volume. Aside from the Loeb versions and a scholarly treatise by the Harvard classicist Kathleen Coleman, I'm not aware of any modern English translation of the sequence as a whole. And the Loeb and Coleman translations are in prose that doesn't particularly serve, and, for me, rather actually works against the poems.

But more on that aspect and on the *Liber Spectaculorum* later. At this point, it serves the reader just to know that my reading of the *Liber Spectaculorum* dissents from the frequent dismissal of this sequence as a simplistic Imperial presentation piece lauding the blood sports of the Colosseum and shamelessly flattering the Flavian dynasty.

Contrarily, I found myself reading a sophisticated sequence whose Latin allows ironies, double-entendres, and – especially – a deeply sardonic voice beneath Martial's surface adulation of the games-presiding "Caesar".

Those who have spent any time with Martial will chime in and say, "of course, that kind of thing is what Martial's all about." I fully agree, and realizing this, I realized that the best – perhaps the only – way to present my "rescued" version of the *Book of the Spectacles* was to frame it in the context of Martial's larger canon. Thus began an extended foray into the "twelve numbered books" of epigrams and a relaxed sampling of the *apophoreta* and *xenia* gift tag couplets. Along with a good deal of peripatetic browsing of often conflicting academic viewpoints on Martial and his literary and political contemporaries.

I also browsed some of the available poetic selections. Particularly those published since the mid-twentieth century relaxation of obscenity laws allowed translators to render Martial's frequent indecencies in English.

And (no surprise to anyone who translates) came to the, obviously opinionated, conclusion that there wasn't any I'd feel enthused to refer a friend to. Each of the small volumes had its merits, but in general, the poet being translated seemed too large and multi-faceted to be that easily captured.

Martial has been highly popular since the Renaissance, but largely in Latin. His short poems are accessible to even a beginning Latin student (and particularly attractive to sophomores in search of smut). So it wasn't until the early 20th century, when Latin left the basic curriculum, that Martial needed to be translated if he was going to be widely read. A perceived priority in the post-1960s translations was to fill the gap left by previously bowdlerized selections. Martial was ideal for those newly liberated times, but I think this also caused less attention to be paid to less salacious poems perceived as already done, resulting in less balanced selections.

The same rush of post-'60s freedom that opened English to Martial also liberated translators to enter into some lively, time-travelling repartee with a poet who seemed as *simpatico* to their brave new era as he was to his own. In his rollicking 1995 selection, entitled *The Mortal City*, William Matthews "enthusiastically opted for anachronisms...", in one case renaming "a greedy Roman mogul Donald Trump, whom I imagine Martial would have delighted to know about." But while Matthews took Martial on an enjoyable tour of 20th century New York, it was at the expense of depriving the reader of Martial's Rome.

In this century, I'm aware of two larger selections: Garry Wills' 2007, highly stylized adaptations, and Susan McLean's 2014 University of Wisconsin volume. Wills' witty readings are in the venerable tradition of "Englishing" that, for Martial, began in the 1600s with Tom Brown's 'Doctor Fell'. But Wills' verse model, not unintentionally, transports the reader more to the aesthetic of 17th and 18th century English epigram, than 1st century C.E. Rome. McLean takes a more literal approach and the volume is informatively notated, but her jaunty, mostly rhyming verse also often has a, decidedly un-Latinate, quasi-limerick feel.

More significantly, both these volumes lack the Latin text. For me, this seems essential if the reader is going to enjoy the sense of illusion that a good *en-face* presentation can afford. Something akin, perhaps, to surtitles in opera. So yes, there is a need for more Martial translation and especially for a balanced selection that has some ambitions toward transporting the reader to Martial's world rather than resurrecting him in an 18th, 19th or 20th century mode.

This selection, I hope, makes some small headway in that direction. But, as I mentioned above, my original aim was to present the *Liber Spectaculorum* Arena poems in the context of Martial's broader poetics. At some point, that limits the size of the selection if the focus on the 37 poem arena sequence is to be maintained. So, the reader shouldn't presume this selection is by any means exhaustive, or – to use that questionable marketing term – an "essential Martial". If anything, it might be characterized as a sort of ''essay in poems'' on Martial, an extended meditation on epigram's protean patron saint and the eternal City he won't let us forget. The reader should also note that, contrary to the usual placement of the *Spectacles* poems at the beginning of Martial's books, I've integrated them in segments between the "numbered books" to give both a sense of trips to the Arena, and of an ongoing work in process. That latter aspect and the uncertain dating of the *Liber Spectaculorum* is discussed at more length in my afterword.

I've also transported my *Xenia* and *Apophoreta* selections from their usual 'Book XIII' and 'Book XIV' placement to "first" place, preceding the selections from the "twelve numbered books" of epigrams. One reason for this is the consensus that these two books appeared in the years prior to *Epigrams, Book I*. More pertinently, these light couplets make a natural appetizer for the fare that follows.

II: SOME HISTORICAL BACKGROUND

Martial was born around 40 C.E., probably during Caligula's reign, and died around 104. If we accept (as Martial did) that Claudius was indeed poisoned by his wife, Aggripina, to hasten her Nero's succession, we might ponder that the first six "Caesars" in Martial's lifetime were violently usurped, with "normalcy" coming only after 69 C.E. "the year of the four emperors".

The first three of these claimants came to violent ends. The last one standing was Vespasian, a grizzled, pragmatic general, with a noted sense of humor. He reigned for ten years and died of natural causes in 79 AD. For the purposes of this selection, it's noteworthy that he built the Colosseum and (as recorded by Suetonius) quipped on his deathbed: *Vae puto, deus fio.* Given Vespasian's involvement in the sacking and destruction of the Jerusalem temple, this might be perversely rendered "Oy, I think I'm becoming a god."

Vespasian's elder son, Titus, succeeded him, but reigned for only two years; beloved by all according to Suetonius, and dying of a fever at the age of 41 in 81. Then came Domitian, his brother. He figures widely in Martial's poems, a somewhat patron, sometimes benefactor, always appropriately flattered. In the "numbered books", the flattery is sometimes obsequious, sometimes playful and subversive. Domitian, the forbearing "lion" to Martial's "hare", someone to be very cautious of while kissing up to. But still teasable as the Emperor / *Censor* who restored (good luck to that!) chastity to Rome.

The level of flattery to the arena games-presiding "Caesar" in the *Spectacles* poems is of another order. More on that later, but as an example of how dangerous Domitian could be, Suetonius notes an incident in the Colosseum when a spectator paid him a compliment he quirkily took as an insult. Domitian had the spectator "dragged from his seat and – with a placard tied around his neck… torn to pieces by dogs in the arena."

Domitian was assassinated in a palace coup in 96, when Martial was 56. Contemporary and near contemporary historians – Tacitus, Suetonius, Cassius Dio – describe a petty, cruel, greedy, and increasingly megalomaniac ruler. Suspicious and manipulative, almost Stalin-like, he cultivated informers to manufacture charges against anyone he might perceive as a threat. Then, routinely did away with the informer, who knew too much. Unlike his father, he was unwilling to wait for *apotheosis* in an afterlife, but came to insist on being addressed while living as "Our Lord and God." In his hubris he renamed the month of September after himself so that he could follow his iconic forbears, Julius Caesar and Augustus, on the calendar.

In time, no one felt safe from Domitian. Especially his closest associates. Finally, his tangled spider web of terror proved too much even for his wife, who joined in the coup. The Senate celebrated his assassination and, instead of the *apotheosis* he anticipated, declared him *damnatio memoriae* rescinding all honorifics bestowed on him. The heads on his statues were replaced with those of others. Even coins bearing his image were recalled and reminted. He was the last of the short Flavian line that began with Vespasian.

Tacitus famously described the rebirth from Domitian's reign in the opening to his *Agricola*: "…as a former age had witnessed the extreme of liberty, so we witnessed the extreme of servitude, when the informer robbed us of the interchange of speech and hearing. We should have lost memory as well as voice, had it been as easy to forget as to keep silence. Now at last our spirit is returning."

Domitian was succeeded by Nerva, the first of the "Five Good Emperors", initiating a period of "imperial meritocracy" marked by nearly a century of stability, growth and prosperity that culminated with Marcus Aurelius. Although Martial managed to survive Domitian, he didn't seem to prosper under the new regime and retired to his native Spain around 98 C.E. He lived another handful of years, missing Rome but claiming to be happy in the country.

III. Translating the Incorrectness of Martial

One question is: How can we ethically enjoy the poetry of a homophobic pederast with a bent for foul language, heartless mockery, blood sports, and animal fights?

We never ask why we enjoy reading and watching dramatizations about Caligula, Nero and the wickedness and intrigues of the early Roman Empire. So what makes the poetry of an exemplar poet – and in some ways an exemplary moralist – of those times any different?

The answer is: It's not different and we do enjoy reading Martial, even when he makes us cringe. We enjoy him in large part because he speaks so directly to us; timelessly honest as it were.

And there's a second level of enjoyment in reading a large enough and varied enough selection of his epigrams. The treat – or *illusion* if you will – of being taken for a stroll around the mean streets and posh villas of Martial's *mea Roma*. A pleasure akin to historical fiction, or more properly, the historical resonance of a unique, primary source voice.

Martial was a younger contemporary of Saint Paul in the Rome that Anthony Burgess characterized, in his 1985 period novel, as *The Kingdom of the Wicked*. But since the Renaissance, literary imagination has been drawn as much, if not more, to Martial's impious Rome than to the Acts of the Apostles. And I think it's that "historical fiction" illusion which has to be pursued if we're going to make peace with Martial's wickedness.

Translated literature endures by mutating across time and cultures. And translated poetry only persists as transplanted poetry, drawing on the soil of a new language, reinventing itself as any immigrant must. Every successful translation is a duet between translator and translatee, an essentially re-authored work. That said (and at the risk of belaboring a point made earlier), I think the wicked banalities of Martial's time particularly resist anachronism whether in images or verse forms.

Their culture's venial sins become, not only mortal, but unforgiveable in our culture. Other than, perhaps, the decried practices of some Afghan warlords, we have no societal model for the routine sexploitation of slave boys, which was seemingly lauded by all, from the Emperor on down. Or for the blood sports, mock-battle slaughters and elaborately staged executions of the Roman Arena, presided over by a munificent Caesar. Beyond that, Martial was also consciously pushing the already indulgent boundaries of 1st century C.E. mores and taste.

But one of the unique beauties of Martial is his ability to forge sinuous, elegant elegiacs from crude, often violent street language and offensive imagery. And from the teeming Roman intersection of sex and economics. Despite his enthusiasm for pederasty, he never lets us forget that he was playing a coercive game enabled by slavery. These poems lose much of their subtlety and too easily turn trivial when they try to emigrate into the classic English epigram model which Martial, ironically, inspired. Their esthetic and, dare I say, ethos are only accessible to us to the extent we can imagine we're reading Latin.

So it's a balancing act. Martial and equally explicit contemporaries like Petronius and Juvenal need to be translated in all their plainspoken up close nakedness. Yet their nudity has to remain exotic. When readers, or translators, try to reimagine them as current day figures, their edginess crosses into transgression, their sinuous satire brays vulgarity.

But why not prose? Can't that be a plain-speaking translator's solution? There are, after all, the Shackleton-Bailey and Walter Ker Loeb complete editions, and a recent prose translation selection by Gideon Nisbet. I'd offer that while prose can be translated poetically, poetry, and particularly the Latin epigram doesn't translate into prose. And, I'll ask Domitian to help me explain.

To wit, Domitian's quip as quoted by Suetonius: *Princeps qui delatores non castigat, irritat.* The correct and usual prose translation is "the prince who does not punish informers, encourages them." But the epigrammatic translation, I think is: "The *princeps* who doesn't whip his informers, spurs them on". This from a ruler routinely depicted on horseback, who was ultimately "thrown" by his subjects.

IV: FORMALITY AND ILLUSION

No one now alive really knows how 1st century Latin was pronounced. And while translators sometimes try to replicate the long and short patterns of Latin verse, the result in English can seem forced and rarely sings. But even for those with minimal Latin, Martial's short poems on the page can convey a transparent sense of musicality and flow. They often innovatively use both internal and end-line rhyme as embellishment, and some even evoke the present day list poem. All this is easy to pick up in the Latin. So my strategy, as I touched on above, is to try to provide a sort of "eye-metric", subtitle accompaniment to the Latin, *en-face* lyric, with the hope of enabling rather than supplanting Martial's voice. This isn't to say the translations are line by line, even when they may look that way. Or that I haven't made liberal use of invisible footnotes and what I think are English equivalent idioms and obscenities.

And of course, that voice remains an imagined voice. The translations I've offered may be somewhat informed, but they're still an imaginative exercise. Compared to modern English with 2,000 more years' worth of words, Martial's Latin vocabulary is a compressed shorthand. Numerous words allow for shades of meaning that allow wide English choices. Beyond that, Martial can be the prince of harmonic polyvalence. My poetic choices are ultimately driven by my own sense of what makes the poem a poem. And some of these will inescapably skew Martial, because the Rome I'm reading is my own imagined Rome.

Scholarship can only assist us in imagining, not knowing Rome. And, if it's to be read for pleasure, historical fiction requires liberties cautious scholarship can't allow. I just hope this selection won't inspire the kind of response Robert Burns gave to a contemporary translator:

O Thou whom Poetry abhors,
Whom Prose has turned out of doors,
Heard'st thou yon groan? – proceed no further,
'Twas laurel'd Martial calling murther.

V: Two Contemporary Views

Martial came to Rome in his twenties, during Nero's notorious reign. Despite Nero's malicious madness, Rome was a thriving, vibrant capitol and a culture on the cusp of its greatest accomplishments. Rome forced Nero to suicide, Nero didn't destroy Rome. Nero, of course, did manage to destroy Martial's fellow Spaniards and putative sponsors, Seneca and

Lucan. But Martial mentions a wide circle of sophisticated friends and patrons. Lucan's widow Polla, Pliny the Younger, the notable grammarian Quintillian, the wealthy aristocrat Arruntius Stella and his wife, a couple he seemed to have a particular bond with. And there was Martial's, not so notable at the time, younger poet friend Juvenal. But despite his gregariousness, we only have one extant contemporary and one, near contemporary mention of Martial.

The first is the famous letter of Pliny the Younger. (The translation is by John Firth, but I've substituted my own translation of the Martial lines Pliny quotes from memory.)

XXX, 21 *to Cornelius Priscus*

I hear that Valerius Martial is dead, and I am much troubled at the news. He was a man of genius, witty and caustic, yet one who in his writings showed as much candour as he did biting wit and ability to sting. When he left Rome I made him a present to help to defray his travelling expenses, as a tribute to the friendship I bore him and to the verses he had composed about me. It was the custom in the old days to reward with offices of distinction or money grants those who had composed eulogies of private individuals or cities, but in our day this custom, like many other honourable and excellent practices, was one of the first to fall into disuse. For when we cease to do deeds worthy of praise, we think it is folly to be praised. Do you ask what the verses are which excited my gratitude? I would refer you to the volume itself, but that I have some by heart, and if you like these, you may look out the others for yourself in the book. He addresses the Muse and bids her seek my house on the Esquiline and approach it with great respect –

> ...But don't get tipsy
> and eager and rap on the counselor's door at a time
> that's not for you. He spends every daylight
> minute agonizing over those luminous
> court orations that posterity will preserve
> and rank with Cicero's. Play it safe and wait
> until the evening lamps are lit. That's your
> special hour; when the wine is poured, when

the rose is queen, when hair's shaken loose.
Then, even grumpy old Catos recite me

Was I not right to take a most friendly farewell of a man who wrote a poem like that about me, and do I do wrong if I now bewail his death as that of a bosom-friend? For he gave me the best he could, and would have given me more if he had had it in his power. And yet what more can be given to a man than glory and praise and immortality? But you may say that Martial's poems will not live for ever. Well, perhaps not, yet at least he wrote them in the hope that they would. Farewell.

The other is an oblique, but apt endorsement by of one of Martial's avid readers a generation or so later: the Emperor Hadrian's adopted son and intended successor, Lucius Celonius Commodus Aelius, also known as "Verus". He never attained the throne because he died around the age of 30 after drinking a suspect potion. The following is from the Loeb translation of the *Historia Augusta*.

Verus was a man of joyous life and well versed in letters, and he was endeared to Hadrian, as the malicious say, rather by his beauty than by his character. In the palace his stay was but a short one; in his private life, though there was little to be commended, yet there was little to be blamed. Furthermore, he was considerate of his family, well-dressed, elegant in appearance, a man of regal beauty, with a countenance that commanded respect, a speaker of unusual eloquence, deft at writing verse, and, moreover, not altogether a failure in public life.

His pleasures, many of which are recorded by his biographers, were not indeed discreditable but somewhat luxurious. For it is Verus who is said to have been the inventor of the *tetrapharmacum*, or rather *pentapharmacum*, of which Hadrian was thereafter always fond, namely, a mixture of sows' udders, pheasant, peacock, ham in pastry and wild boar…

There was also another kind of pleasure, it is said, of which Verus was the inventor. He constructed, namely, a bed provided with four high cushions and all inclosed with a fine net; this he filled with rose-leaves, from which the white parts had been removed, and then reclined on it with his mistresses, burying himself under a coverlet made of lilies, himself anointed with perfumes from Persia. Some even relate that he made couches and tables of roses and lilies, these flowers all carefully cleansed, a practice, which, if not creditable, at least did not make for the destruction of the state.

Furthermore, he always kept the *Recipes* of Caelius Apicius and also Ovid's *Amores* at his bedside, *and declared that Martial, the writer of Epigrams, was his Vergil.* ...And when his wife complained about his amours with others, he said to her, it is reported: "Let me indulge my desires with others; for wife is a term of honour, not of pleasure."

Unlike the cautious Pliny, Aelius seems to have had no doubts about how long Martial's poems would live.

THE POEMS

The Latin text and organization is based on the current David Shackleton Bailey, Loeb edition. That version and predecessor versions delineate the *Xenia* and *Apophoreta* sequences as "Books XIII and XIV", placing them at the end of Martial's XII books of *Epigrams*. But this is an editorial, not chronological placement. The current scholarly consensus is that the *Xenia* (gift tags for presents to banquet guests) and *Apophoreta* (Saturnalia gift tags) preceded the publication of the *Epigrams*. As discussed above and in the afterword, my reasons for integrating the *Liber Spectaculorum* in twelve segments are also editorial, not chronological.

The dating of the individual books remains an ongoing topic of technical discussion. Just as a convenient guide, I've used the chronology offered by Kathleen Coleman in a 2005 *Acta Classica* article.

BOOK XIII "XENIA"
Saturnalia 83/84 c.e.

XIII, 4 *Tus*

Serus ut aetheriae Germanicus imperet aulae
    utque diu terris da pia tura Iovi.

XIII, 29 *Vas Damascenorum*

Pruna peregrinae carie rugosa senectae
    sume: solent duri solvere ventris onus.

XIII, 34 *Bulbi*

Cum sit anus coniunx et sint tibi mortua membra,
    nil aliud bulbis quam satur esse potes.

XIII, 48 *Boleti*

Argentum atque aurum facile est laenamque togamque
    mittere: boletos mittere difficile est.

XIII, 92 *Lepores*

Inter aves turdus, si quid me iudice certum est
    inter quadripedes mattea prima lepus.

XIII, 4 *Incense*

So that *Germanicus* may eventually rule in heavenly halls,
  and on earth for many days, offer holy incense to Jove.

(*Germanicus* here refers to a soubriquet assumed by Domitian after defeating a minor
German tribe. He also renamed the month of September *Germanicus* to honor himself.)

XIII, 29 *Jar of Damask Prunes*

Accept these wrinkled, dried, old exotic plums. They
  have a way of loosening the load of a stopped up gut.

XIII, 34 *Onions*

When your wife is old and your member wilts,
  satisfaction only comes from gobbling onions.

XIII, *Mushrooms*

It's easy to send silver, or gold, or a nice cloak, or
  a toga: but mushrooms are difficult to part with.

XIII, 92

As far as birds, the thrush is surely, if I'm any judge,
  the daintiest dish. But on four legs, it's rabbit.

BOOK XIV "APOPHORETA"
Saturnalia 84/85

XIV, 6 *Triplices*

Tunc triplices nostros non vilia dona putabis,
   cum se venturam scribet amica tibi.

XIV, 39 *Lucerna cubicularis*

Dulcis conscia lectuli lucerna,
quidquid vis facias licet, tacebo.

XIV, 63 *Tibiae*

Ebria non madidis rumpit tibicina buccis;
   saepe duas pariter; saepe monaulon habet.

XIV, 107 *Calathi.*

Nos Satyri, nos Bacchus amat, nos ebria tigris,
   Perfusos domini lambere docta pedes.

XIV, 134 *Fascia pectoralis*

Fascia, crescentes dominae compesce papillas,
   ut sit quod capiat nostra tegatque manus.

XIV, 165 *Cithara*

Reddidit Eurydicen vati: sed perdidit ipse,
   dum sibi non credit nec patienter amat.

XIV, 6 *Three-leaved tablets*

You won't think this little notepad is such a cheap present
   when your girlfriend writes you that she's on her way.

XIV, 39 *Bedroom Lamp*

I am an oil lamp, your sweet bed's accomplice.
You can do whatever you'd like, I won't talk.

XIV, 63 *Double Aulos Pipes*

The drunken flautist blows us with her dripping cheeks.
   Sometimes she has two together, sometimes a single pipe.

XIV, 107 *Flaskets*

Satyrs love us, Bacchus loves us, as does the tippling
   tigress trained to lick her master's sodden feet.

XIV, 134 *Breastband*

Sash, restrain my lady's swelling nipples,
   so they can nestle in our hands.

XIV, 165 *Lyre*

It returned Eurydice to the great poet: but then he lost her.
   Because he loved with neither trust nor patience

LIBER SPECTACULORUM
The Book of the Spectacles (dating uncertain)

Sp. 1.

Barbara pyramidum sileat miracula Memphis
    Assyrius iactet nec Babylona labor,
nec Triviae templo molles laudentur Iones,
    dissimulet Delon cornibus ara frequens;
aere nec vacuo pendentia Mausolea
    laudibus immodicis Cares in astra ferant.
omnis Caesareo cedit labor Amphitheatro:
    unum pro cunctis fama loquetur opus.

Sp. 2.

Hic ubi sidereus propius videt astra colossus
    et crescunt media pegmata celsa via,
invidiosa feri radiabant atria regis
    unaque iam tota stabat in urbe domus.

hic ubi conspicui venerabilis Amphitheatri
    ergitur moles, stagna Neronis erant.
hic ubi miramur, velocia munera thermas,
    abstulerat miseris tecta superbus ager.

Claudia diffusas ubi porticus explicat umbras,
    ultima pars aulae deficientis erat.
reditta Roma, sibi est et sunt te praeside, Caesar,
    deliciae populi, quae fuerant domini.

Sp. 1.

Barbarous Memphis, bite your tongue about those
miraculous pyramids. Assyrians, stop glorifying
old Babylon's murmuring gardens. And you, effete
Ionians, enough gushing over Artemis' Temple.

The Altar of Many Horns lies overgrown on abandoned Delos,
and it's only a Mausoleum suspended in the empty air that
Halicarnassus insists on praising to the stars.

With Caesar's Amphitheater, all these efforts fade away:
One great work that brings everything else to fruition,
that's what history will say.

Sp. 2.

Here – where the Colossus peers with sparkling eyes right up
    into the stars and tall scaffolds soar high over the concourse –
there once glowered the glittering mansion of a spiteful
    king. In all of the City, only his house mattered.

Here – where the venerated amphitheater rises on its
    pilings for all to see – Nero's pools once brooded.
Here – where we marvel at your gift of the public baths, so readily
    bestowed – his arrogance razed the humble homesteads of the poor.

But that cruel palace never reached beyond the boundary
    where the shady portico of the Claudian Colonnade ends.
Rome has been given back to herself and, under your charge,
    Caesar, the people enjoy the pleasures of their former master.

Sp. 3.

Qaue tam seposita est, quae gens tam barbara, Caesar,
  ex qua spectator non sit in urbe tua?

venit ab Orpheo cultor Rhodopeius Haemo,
  venit et epoto Sarmata pastas equo,

et qui prima bibit deprensi flumina Nili,
  et quem suprema Tethyos unda ferit.

festinavit Arabs, festinavere Sabei,
  et Ciliices nimbis hic maduere suis.

crinibus in nodum tortis venere Sygambri,
  atque aliter tortis crinibus Aethiopes.

vox diversa sonat populorum, tum tamen una est,
  cum verus patriae diceres esse pater.

Sp. 3.

What race is so far-flung or barbarous, Caesar,
    that it doesn't send a spectator to your City:

A farmer from Rhodope and Haemus, Orpheus' green mountains,
    alongside a Sarmatian nomad raised to subsist on his horse's blood.

A traveler whose first drink was from the headwaters of the Nile.
    And another on whose bleak shore the farthest waves of Tethys crash.

The Arabs come hurrying, the Sabaens scurrying,
    and the Cilicians arrive to a weloming shower of saffron.

Sicambrians, their blond hair kinked in knots,
    mingle with Ethiopians with their own kinky hair.

A population speaking a babble of tongues, but they harmonize
    into one voice that proclaims you the Fatherland's true Father.

EPIGRAMS, BOOK I
Late 85, early 86 c.e.

I, 4

Contigeris nostros, Caesar, si forte libellos,
  terrarum dominum pone supercilium.
consuevere iocos vestri quoque ferre triumphi,
  materiam dictis nec pudet esse ducem.
qua Thymelen spectas derisoremque Latinum,
  illa fronte precor carmina nostra legas.
innocuos censura potest permittere lusus:
  lasciva est nobis pagina, vita proba.

I, 6

Aetherias aquila puerum portante per auras
  illaesum timidis unguibus haesit onus:
nunc sua Caesareos exorat praeda leones
  tutus et ingenti ludit in ore lepus.
quae maiore putas miraculis? summus utrisque
  auctor adest haec sunt Caesarism illa Iovis.

I, 13

Casta suo gladium cum traderet Arria Paeto,
  quem de visceribus strinxerat ipsa suis,
'Si qua fides, vulnus quod feci non dolet,' inquit,
  'sed tu quod facies, hoc mihi, Paete, dolet.'

I, 4

If you chance upon my book Caesar, relax the raised
   eyebrows that govern the world. *Triumphators* have
to endure rude jokes. And commanders aren't shamed
   by their troops' coarse marching chants. Read my
poems with the smile you can't help when watching
   Thymele and that scamp Latinus in the mime show:
A *Censor* is allowed some harmless fun. My pages
   are shameless, an honest living.

I, 6

The great eagle carried Ganymede, unharmed, through
   windy heavens, its fearsome talons anxious for their burden.
Now, Caesar's lions are similarly charmed by their prey,
   and hares hop in play through enormous yawning jaws.
Which do you think more marvelous, lions or eagle? Both
   answer to the highest. One to Caesar, the other, Jupiter.

I, 13

As Arria, that good wife, passed Paetus the blade
   she'd pulled from her own vitals, she gasped
"so hard to believe how little it hurts. Watching
   you follow, husband, that's what hurts."

(Caecina Paetus was condemned to death by the Emperor Claudius in 42 C.E. He had
the choice of suicide but faltered. His lifelong wife Arria opted to assist and join him.)

I, 21

Cum peteret regem, decepta satellite dextra
   ingessit sacris se peritura focis.
sed tam saeva pius miracula non tulit hostis
   et raptum flammis iussit abire virum:
urere quam potuit contempto Mucius igne.
   hanc spectare manum Porsena non potuit.
maior deceptae fama est et gloria dextrae:
   si non errasset fecerat illa minus.

I, 23

Invitas nullam nisi cum quo, Cotta, lavaris
   et dant convivam balnea sola tibi.
mirabar quare numquam me, Cotta, vocasses:
   iam scio me nudum displicuisse tibi.

I, 24

Aspicis incomptis illum, Deciane, capillis,
   cuius et ipse times triste supercilium,
qui loquitur Curios adsertoresque Camillos?
   Nolito fronti credere: nupsit heri.

I, 32

Non amo te, Sabidi, nec possum dicere quare:
   hoc tantum possum dicere, non amo te.

I, 21

The sword hand that meant to kill the king, was fooled
 by his regal attendant. So it calmly endured its own ruin
held in the sacred flame. But the pious adversary couldn't
 stomach the savage display. He pulled the hero from the flames
and sent him on his way. The hand Mucius so contemptuously
 burned, Porsena couldn't bear to look at. The right hand whose
blunder won more glory than Mucius ever envisioned.
 If it hadn't gone astray, it would have achieved much less.

I, 23

You don't invite anyone you haven't bathed
 with, Cotta. You fill your guest list at the baths.
I used to wonder why you never asked me to dinner:
 I must not be that appetizing with my clothes off.

I, 24

Do you see that guy with rough shaggy hair, Decianus,
 the one so somber, intimidating and haughty, trotting
out the peoples' heroes and those yesteryear virtues? I
 wouldn't trust his looks. Yesterday, he became a bride.

I, 32

I don't love you, Sabidius, I can't even say
 why. I can only say, I don't love you.

(This poem is the inspiration for Tom Brown's "I Do not Love Thee Dr. Fell". But it's
also widely commented on as Martial's light riff on Catullus 85: And perhaps gives us
yet another way to read that endlessly fertile couplet:
Odi et amo. quare id faciam, fortasse requiris. I hate you, love you, ask me, I don't know why
nescio, sed fieri sentio et excrucior.   I only know what I feel, and I'm crucified)

.

I, 35

Versus scribere me parum severos
nec quos praelegat in schola magister,
Corneli, quereris: sed hi libelli,
tamquam coniugibus suis mariti,
non possunt sine mentula placere.

Quid si me iubeas thalassionem
uerbis dicere non thalassionis?
quis Floralia vestit et stolatum
permittit meretricibus pudorem?
Lex haec carminibus data est iocosis,

ne possint, nisi pruriant, iuvare.
Quare deposita severitate
parcas lusibus et iocis rogamus,
nec castrare velis meos libellos:
Gallo turpis est nihil Priapo.

I, 37

Ventris onus misero, nec te pudet, excipis auro,
   Basse, bibis vitro: carius ergo cacas.

I, 42

Coniugis audisset fatum cum Porcia Bruti
   et subtracta sibi quareret arma dolor,
'Nondum scitis' ait 'mortem non posse negari?
   credideram fatis hoc docuisse patrem.'
Dixit et ardentis avido bibit ore favillas.
   I nunc et ferrum, turba molesta, nega.

I, 35

You don't deem my verses proper
enough, Cornelius, not the kind of thing
a teacher recites to his class. But these
little books are, so to speak, like husbands
who can only satisfy their wives with a cock.

Are you telling me to sing wedding
songs without wedding song words?
What kind of prudes bundle up
under robes at the *Florialia* where
whores dance free? The law is that

harmless poems are charmless unless
they gratify a certain itch. So spare me
your rectitude, just laugh at my jokes.
Don't try to castrate my books. Nothing's
more obscene than a limp, neutered *Priapus*.

I, 37

You dump your belly's burden, Bassus, in a grimacing gold chamber pot.
    And toast yourself with a water glass, while your money goes to shit.

I, 42

When Porcia learned, her husband, Brutus' fate, she
    searched in her grief for the weapons they'd removed.
"Don't you understand yet? You can't deny death",
    she seethed. "Didn't father's stubborn ending prove
that?" Then she greedily gulped down hot glowing
    coals. Go ahead, you meddling fools, deny cold steel.

(Portia's father was Cato the Younger, another famous "principled" suicide.)

I, 46

Cum dicis 'Propero, fac si facis,' Hedyle, languet
  protinus et cessat debilitata Venus.
Expectare iube: velocius ibo retentus.
  Hedyle, si properas, dic mihi ne properem.

I, 57

Qualem, Flacce, velim quaeris nolimque puellam?
  nolo nimis facilem difficilemque nimis.
Illud quod medium est atque inter utrumque probamus:
  nec volo quod cruciat nec volo quod satiat.

I, 77

Pulchre valet Charinus et tamen pallet.
parce bibit Charinus et tamen pallet.
bene concoquit Charinus et tamen pallet.
sole utitur Charinus et tamen pallet.
tingit cuten Charinus et tamen pallet.
cunnum Charinus lingit et tamen pallet.

I, 46

When you say "I'm coming, do it if you're going to",
   Hedylus, I wilt and desire suddenly deserts me. But
whine "slow down", and I just go faster. Hedylus,
   if you want me to come, beg me not to.

(As in many of Martial's "boy love" poems, a reader might reasonably assume
   that Hedylus is the speaker's slave.)

I, 57

You ask, Flaccus, what kind of girl I like, what kind
   I avoid? Someone not too easy, not too maddening.
The golden mean lies somewhere in between.
   I don't want agony. I don't want too much.

(Some also link this poem to Catullus 85 because of the last line *cruciat* image. *Flacce*
   may be Martial's friend Flaccus, but also evokes another Flaccus, i.e. Horace and his
   Ode II, 10.)

I, 77

Charinus is in perfect health, and yet he's pale.
Charinus barely imbibes, and yet he's pale.
Charinus has a fine digestion, and yet he's pale.
Charinus spends the day in the sun, and yet he's pale.
Charinus tries wearing rouge, and he's still pale.
Pale face Charinus, licks cunt and barely blushes.

I, 78

Indignas premeret pestis cum tabida fauces
    inque ipsos vultus serperet atra lues,
siccis ipse genis flentes hortatus amicos
    decrevit Stygios Festus adire lacus.
nec tamen obscuro pia polluit ora veneno
    aut torsit lenta tristia fata fame,
sanctam Romana vitam sed morte peregit
    dimistique animam nobiliore rogo.
hanc mortem fatis magni praeferre Catonis
    fama potest: huius Caesar amicus erat.

I, 83

Os et labra tibi lingit, Manneia, catellus:
    non miror, merdas si libet esse cani.

I, 88

Alcime, quem raptum domino crescentibus annis
    Labicana levi caespite velat humus,
accipe non Pario nutantia pondera saxo,
    quae cineri uanus dat ruitura labor,
sed faciles buxos et opacas palmitis umbras
    quaeque virent lacrimis roscida prata meis
accipe, care puer, nostri monimenta doloris:
    hic tibi perpetuo tempore vivet honor.
Cum mihi supremos Lachesis perneverit annos,
    non aliter cineres mando iacere meos.

I, 78

An undeserved malignancy fed on his throat,
  and dark disease began to snake into his face.
Dry eyed himself but consoling his weeping friends,
  Festus chose to depart to the Stygian pools.
He didn't pollute his pious lips with subtle
  poison, nor drag things out with slow starvation, but
ended a virtuous life with a Roman death,
  liberating his soul with a quick noble act.
A death even more talked about than great Cato's
  example: because Festus was a *Friend of Caesar*.

(Festus has been likely identified as C. Valerius Festus, a member of Domitian's inner
  circle advisory council, the *Amici Caesaris*. His complicity in the murder of his
  brother-in-law was instrumental in Vespasian's coming to power.)

I, 83

Your adorable puppy loves licking your face and lips,
  Manneia. No surprise. Dogs even like to eat shit.

I, 88

Stolen from your master in the ripeness of youth,
  Alcimus; you lie gently hidden now by grassy earth
beside the Labicana Way. Don't envy the sinking weight
  of marble gravestones, those labored memorials
to ruin and futility. Take your ease here among vine
  buds shaded by boxwood, in this green little plot
watered by the dew of my tears. Accept, treasured lad,
  this monument of our sorrow which honors you
with timeless, perpetual life. When Lachesis spins out my
  own final years, I want no other sleep for my ashes.

I, 89

Garris in aurem semper omnibus, Cinna,
garrire et illud teste quod licet turba.
rides in aurem, quereris, arguis, ploras,
cantas in aurem, indicas, taces, clamas,
adeoque penitus sedit hic tibi morbus,
ut saepe in aurem, Cinna, Caesarem laudes.

I. 94

Cantasti male, dum fututa es, Aegle.
Iam cantas bene: basianda non es.

I, 101

lla manus quondam studiorum fida meorum
    et felix domino notaque Caesaribus,
destituit primos viridis Demetrius annos:
    quarta tribus lustris addita messis erat.
Ne tamen ad Stygias famulus descenderet umbras,
    ureret implicitum cum scelerata lues,
cauimus et domini ius omne remisimus aegro:
    munere dignus erat convaluisse meo.
Sensit deficiens sua praemia meque patronum
    dixit ad infernas liber iturus aquas.

I, 89

You're always blabbing in someone's ear, Cinna,
whispering what the crowd already knows.
You joke, complain, argue, deplore, and sing,
inform, hint, and proclaim – confidentially.
This illness could be serious Cinna. You're even
praising Caesar, now, like a secret, lips to ear.

I. 94

You sang poorly then, you only knew how to fuck, Aegle.
Now you positively warble, but you're not to be kissed.

I, 101

Demetrius – whose faithful penmanship
    captured his master's eager verse in a hand
even the Caesars recognized – is gone. In the
    very bloom of youth, plucked in the autumn of
his twentieth year. Tangled in fever and gnawed
    by plague, I couldn't let him descend to the caverns
of the Styx a slave. I ceded my rights, praying
    the ceremony might somehow even heal him.
He sensed the gift, smiled, whispered *Patron,*
    and embarked, free on those sunless waters.

I, 107

Saepe mihi dicis, Luci carissime Iuli,
    'scribe aliquid magnum: desidiosus homo es.'
Otia da nobis, sed qualia fecerat olim
    Maecenas Flacco Vergilioque suo:
condere victuras temptem per saecula curas
    et nomen flammis eripuisse meum.
In steriles nolunt campos iuga ferre iuuenci:
    pingue solum lassat, sed iuvat ipse labor.

I, 107

Yes, tell me again, cousin Lucius dear Julius,
    "Write something really big, stir those lazy bones."
Well, give me some real leisure, the kind Maecenas
    once crafted for his Horace and Virgil as their gift
to use. Then I'd be tempted to generate an opus
    for the ages and snatch my own name from the pyre.
Yoked oxen hate plowing fruitless fields. Rich earth
    wearies as well, but the work is pleasure itself

Sp. 4.

Turba gravis paci placidaeque inimica quieti,
    quae semper miseras sollicitabat opes,
traducta est, ingens nec cepit harena nocentis:
    et delator habet quod dabat exilium.

Sp. 5.

Exulat Ausonia profugus delator ab urbe:
    haec licet inpensis principes adnumeres.

Sp. 4.

That mob that strained peace and hated order,
   constantly harassing and ruining their betters,
is trooped out, and the arena can barely hold the guilty:
   As one informer after another is granted his own exile.

Sp. 5.

The informant absconds into exile from City and Homeland;
   charge the loss to the *princeps'* account.

BOOK II
Late 86, early 87 C.E..

II, 18

Capto tuam, pudet heu, sed capto, Maxime, cenam,
    tu captas aliam: iam sumus ergo pares.
Mane salutatum venio, tu diceris isse
    ante salutatum: iam sumus ergo pares.
Sum comes ipse tuus tumidique anteambulo regis,
    tu comes alterius: iam sumus ergo pares.
Esse sat est servum, iam nolo vicarius esse.
    Qui rex est regem, Maxime, non habeat.

II, 33

Cur non basio te, Philaeni? calva es.
Cur non basio te, Philaeni? rufa es.
Cur non basio te, Philaeni? lusca es.
Haec qui basiat, o Philaeni, fellat.

II, 48

Coponem laniumque balneumque
tonsorem tabulamque calculosque
et paucos, sed ut eligam, libellos:
unum non nimium rudem sodalem
et grandem puerum diuque levem
et caram puero meo puellam:
haec praesta mihi, Rufe, vel Butuntis,
et thermas tibi have Neronianas.

II, 18

I wheedle, shamelessly, for a spot on your guest list, Maximus.
   You're kissing up to someone else. So, in this, we're equals.
I arrive to pay my morning respects. But you're out, calling
   on patrons yourself. So, we're equals in that respect.
I walk ahead on your rounds, clearing the way like a lackey
   for some pompous princeling. You do the same for someone else.
Once again, we're a pair. It's bad enough being a slave, I'm
   not going to serve one. A king, Maximus, doesn't have a king.

II, 33

Why don't I kiss you, Philaenus? You're so bald.
Why don't I kiss you, Philaenus? You're beet red.
Why don't I kiss you, Philaenus? You're one-eyed.
Only a cocksucker, dear Philaenus, would kiss you.

II, 48

A bartender and a butcher, a bath and
a barber. A game board with pieces,
and my own small selection of books.
One not too boorish friend. A big strong
boy still years from his beard, and a girl
to my boy's liking. Give me these, Rufus,
even in some nowhere town, and you can
keep Nero's grand, steaming pools.

II, 51

Unus saepe tibi tota denarius arca
   cum sit et hic culo tritior, Hylle, tuo,
non tamen hunc pistor, non auferet hunc tibi copo,
   sed si quis nimio pene superbus erit.
Infelix uenter spectat convivia culi,
   et semper miser hic esurit, ille vorat.

II, 52

Novit loturos Dasius numerare: poposcit
   mammosam Spatalen pro tribus; illa dedit.

II, 53

Vis fieri liber? Mentiris, Maxime, non vis:
   sed fieri si vis, hac ratione potes.
Liber eris, cenare foris si, Maxime, nolis,
   Veintana tuam si domat uva sitim,
si ridere potes miseri chrysendeta Cinnae, 5
   contentus nostra si potes esse toga,
si plebeia Venus gemino tibi vincitur asse,
   si tua non rectus tecta subire potes.
Haec tibi si vis est, si mentis tanta potestas,
   liberior Partho vivere rege potes.

II, 82

Abscisa servum quid figis, Pontice lingua?
   necsis tu populum, quod tacet ille, loqui?

II, 51

So often, your money box is down to one *denarius*,
    and that rubbed smoother than your butt, Hyllus.
But you don't surrender it to the baker or the bartender;
    you find someone peddling a truly superb sausage.
And your unhappy belly glowers at your feasting
    asshole, starving, while that glutton gorges.

II, 52

Dasius, the bath attendant, knows his numbers. He told Spatala
    her bazooms were so big she owed for three. She came across.

II, 53

You want to escape it all? You say so Maximus,
    but don't. If you really did, here's how it's done.
Be your own master; stop chasing dinner invitations;
    let humble tavern wine quell your thirst. Resist
the glitter of ridiculous Cinna's gold plated tableware.
    Try on my toga for size: Let yourself be captivated
by the plebeian heaven of an ordinary two bit whore.
    So what if your doorway makes you stoop: If
you really want it, if you have a mind to, and strength
    enough, you can live as free as Persian royalty.

II, 82

Ponticus, so you cut your slave's tongue out and crucified him.
    Can't you hear the whole city now, whispering what he can't tell?

II, 83

Foedaste miserum, marite, moechum,
et se, qui fuerant prius, requirunt
trunci naribus auribusque vultus.
credis te satis esse vindicatum?
erras: iste potest et irrumari.

II, 87

Dicis amore tui bellas ardere puellas,
    qui faciem sub aqua, Sexte, natantis habes.

II, 89

Quod nimio gaudes noctem producere vino
    ignosco: vitium, Gaure, Catonis habes.
Carmina quod scribis Musis et Apolline nullo
    laudari debes: hoc Ciceronis habes.
Quod vomis, Antoni: quod luxuriaris, Apici.
    Quod fellas, vitium dic mihi cuius habes?

II, 83

You really mangled your wife's
whimpering lover. Let him go chase his
lost looks – and his missing ears and nose.
Retribution. But satisfaction? Not
until you make him suck you off.

(For Latinists familiar with this sometimes variously interpreted poem, my translation
  follows UCLA classicist, Amy Richlin's reading and her amendment of *irrumare* to
  irrumari.)

II, 87

You sputter about all the cuties boiling with love for you, Sextus, with
the face of a man swimming underwater.

II, 89

As far as carousing the night away with too much wine,
    Gaurus, we can excuse that same failing Cato had.
And you should be praised for writing clumsy pedestrian
    verse: Cicero did too. You waste a fortune on exotic
food, as did Apicius. And puke, just like Marc Antony.
    But what great Roman inspired you to suck cock?

Sp. 6.

Iunctam Pasiphaen Dictaeo credite tauro:
   vidimus, accepit fabula prisca fidem.
nec se miratur, Caesar, longaeva vetustas:
   quidquid fama canit, praestat harena tibi.

Sp. 7.

Belliger invictis quod Mars tibi servit in armis,
   non satis est, Caesar; servit et ipsa Venus.

Sp. 8.

Prostratum vasta Nemees in valle leonem
   nobilis Herculeum fama canebat opus.
prisca fides taceat: nam post tua munera, Caesar.
   haec iam femines vidimus acta manu.

Sp. 6.

That Pasiphae coupled with the Cretan bull – believe it!
　We've seen it: the fable we used to have to take on faith.
You shouldn't be surprised, Caesar, at such an old tale retold.
　Whatever myth sings, the arena presents you with.

Sp. 7.

It's not enough that Mars, the invincible warrior, performs
　at your command, Caesar. Venus attends you as well.

Sp. 8.

The old myths extol Hercules' great labors and the Nemean
　lion brought to earth in a wilderness valley. But forget
those ancient ovations. Now, you've given us the
　Games, Caesar – and we can see this is just woman's work.

BOOK III
87 / 88 c.e.

III, 17

Circumlata diu mensis scribilita secundis
   urebat nimio saeva calore manus;
sed magis ardebat Sabidi gula: protinus ergo
   sufflavit buccis terque quaterque suis.
Illa quidem tepuit digitosque admittere visa est,
   sed nemo potuit tangere: merda fuit.

III, 65

Quod spirat tenera malum mordente puella,
   quod de Corycio quae venit aura croco;
vinea quod primis cum floret cana racemis,
   gramina quod redolent, quae modo carpsit ovis;
quod myrtus, quod messor Arabs, quod sucina trita,
   pallidus Eoo ture quod ignis olet;
gleba quod aestivo leviter cum spargitur imbre,
   quod madidas nardo passa corona comas:
hoc tua, saeve puer Diadumene, basia fragrant.
    Quid si tota dares illa sine invidia?

III, 75

Stare, Luperce, tibi iam pridem mentula desit,
   luctaris demens tu tamen arrigere.
Sed nihil erucae faciunt bulbique salaces,
   inproba nec prosunt iam satureia tibi.
Coepisti puras opibus corrumpere buccas:
   sic quoque non vivit sollicitata Venus.
Mirari satis hoc quisquam vel credere possit,
   quod non stat, magno stare, Luperce, tibi?

III, 17

The steaming cheese tart was so hot it burned our hands;
    as we gingerly tossed it, back and forth, around the table.
Then Sabidius' eager gullet glowed. Puffing out his cheeks,
    he blew on the treat, three, four times. Until it turned
lukewarm, and finally seemed safe for our fingers. As
    if anyone would touch it, now that it was shit.

III, 65

The sweet gasp of an apple as a young girl bites
    into it. The ephemeral scent of Corycian saffron,
Spring vineyards white with buds and grass
    that sheep have freshly grazed. A musky
harvest of Arabian spice, myrtle, rubbed amber,
    and incense lit to welcome the pale dawn.
The odor of earth sprinkled by a brief summer rain.
    Tresses fragrant with sweat and balsam. Your kisses,
fierce Diadumenus boy, evoke all these. What would
    all this be like if you could give them without hatred?

III, 75

Your prick gave up on itself, long ago, Lupercus,
    but the struggle to revive it consumes you.
Kale and lustful onions do nothing. Shameless
    savory isn't any use. Now, (can anyone
make sense of this?) you're offering outrageous
    premiums for innocent virgins, hoping their shy
mouths can arouse a response. What's worthless
    is costing you your fortune, Lupercus.

III, 83

Ut faciem breviora mones epigrammata, Corde.
　'fac mihi quod Chione' : non putui brevius.

III, 84

Quid narrat tua moecha? non puellam
dixi, Gongylion, quid ergo? linguam.

III, 87

Narrat te rumor, Chione, numquam esse fututam
　atque nihil cunno purius esse tuo.
tacta tamen non hac, qua debes, parte lavaris:
　si pudor est, transfer subligar in faciem.

III, 96

Lingis, non futuis meam puellam
et garris quam moechus fututor.
et te prendero, Gargili, tacebus.

III, 97

Ne legat hunc Chione, mando tibi Rufe, libellum.
　carmine laesa meo est: laedere et illa potest..

III, 83

You think my epigrams should be shorter, Cordus? Well just
    "do for me, what Chione does". I can't finish more quickly than that.

III, 84

What does your wife's queer lover have to say?
Not the girl, Gongylion, I mean your tongue.

III, 87

Chione, as rumor has it, you've never been fucked,
    and nothing is purer than your cunt. You even wade
into the baths covered up – but not the right part.
    Shame on you, pull that underwear up over your face.

III, 96

So my girl let you lick her cunt; now you're
bragging you're her fucking lover. Just
let me catch you, Gargilius. I'll give you
a mouthful that'll shut you up.

III, 97

I'm telling you Rufus, we can't let Chione read this book.
    My poems took a real bite out of her. She might just bite back.

Sp, 9.

Qualiter in Scythica religatus rupe Prometheus
    adsiduam nimio pectore pavit avem,
nudo Caledonio sic viscera praebuit urso
    non falsa pendens in cruce Laureolus.
vivebant laceri membris stillantibus artus
    inque omni nusquam corpore corpus erat.

denique suppliciam ....
    vel domini iugulam foderat ense nocens,
templa vel arcano demens spoliaverat auro,
    subdiderat saevas vel tibi, Roma, faces.
vicerant antiquae sceleratus crimina famae,
    in quo, quae fuerant fabula, poena fuit.

Sp, 10.

Daedale, Lucano cum sic lacereris ab urso,
    quam cuperes pinnas nunc habuisse tuas!

Sp, 9.

So, oddly, reminiscent of Prometheus chained
  to the Scythian crags with the relentless bird gorging
on his too-big heart. The guy acting the part of the mime
  show bandit, Laureolus. Naked, helpless, hanging on
no make believe cross, and offering up his guts to
  a Caledonian bear. His torn apart parts, dripping. Joints
still writhing alive in a body no longer anyone's body.

  Justice at last. (But tell me again what he did?)
Did his guilty sword slit his master's throat? Or
  did the harebrain burgle a temple looking for secret gold?
Or maybe this savage was even plotting to put you –
  gentle Rome – to the torch? Does it matter?.
He's certainly outdone the old storybook desperados.
  Their crimes are fables; his punishment, the real thing.

Sp, 10.

Oh, "Daedalus", how you yearn for wings now –
  while the Lucanian bear tears into you…

BOOK IV
Saturnalia 88 c.e.

IV, 7

Cur here quod dederas, hodie, puer Hylle, negasti,
   durus tam subito, qui modo mitis eras?
sed iam causaris barbamque annosque pilosque.
   o nox, quam longa es, quae facis una senem!
quid nos derides? here qui puer, Hylle, fuisti,
   dic nobis, hodie qua ratione vir es?

IV, 17

Facere in Lyciscam Paule, me iubes versus,
quibus illa lectis rubeat et sit irata,
O Paule, malus es: irrumare vis solus.

IV, 20

Dicit se vetulam, cum sit Caerellia pupa:
   pupam se dicit Gellia, cum sit anus.
Ferre nec hanc possis, possis, Colline, nec illam:
   altera ridicula est, altera putidula.

IV, 21

Nullos esse deos, inane caelum
affirmat Segius: probatque, quod se
factum, dum negat haec, videt beatum.

IV, 7

What you gave me yesterday, you say "no" to today,
  young Hyllus, so suddenly tough, so recently submissive.
Now you plead your fuzzy beard and even body hairs.
  What a long, long night that was to turn you into a codger.
Why are you smirking? You were just a boy yesterday,
  Hyllus; tell us – what impulse made a man of you?

IV, 17

Paulus, you want me to write verses about Lycisca –
the kind that, when she reads them, will make her
blush, then scream with rage. Oh Paulus, you're bad.
You just want to be the only prick in her mouth

IV, 20

Caerellia says she's "grandma", but she's just a baby doll.
  "Baby Doll" is what that fossil Gellia calls herself.
One can indulge the former, not the latter, Collinus.
  One's laughable, the other's a sick joke.

IV, 21

The gods don't exist. Just a lie in the sky,
Segius thunders. Self-evident, undeniable.
How else could he get so blessed rich?

IV, 38

Galla, nega; satiatur amor nisi gaudia torquent:
    sed noli nimium, Galla, negare diu.

IV, 44

Hic est pampineis viridis modo Vesbius umbris,
    presserat hic madidos nobilis uva lacus:
haec iuga quam Nysae colles plus Bacchus amavit,
    hoc nuper Satyris monte dedere choros.
haec Veneris sedes, Lacedaemone gratior illi.
    hic locus Herculeo nomine clarus erat.
cuncta iacent flammis et tristi mersa favilla
    nec superi vellent hoc licuisse sibi.

IV, 48

Percidi guades, percisus, Papyle, ploras.
    cur quae vis fieri, Papyle, facta doles?
paenitet obscenae pruriginis? an magis illud
    fles, quod percidi, Papyle, desieris?

Book IV, 50

Quid me, Thai, senem subinde dicis?
nemo est, Thai, senex ad irrumendum.

IV, 38

All right Galla, say no: Love needs a little struggle to satisfy.
    But just a little, Galla: Don't keep this up all day

IV, 44

Remember Vesuvius, so green, so vine shaded, its
    wine presses overflowing with noble grapes. Bacchus
came to love those ridges more than his childhood Nysa hills,
    this mountain where elusive satyrs were said to dance and
sing. And Venus preferred its slopes to her Spartan temple,
    as she lingered in the breeze above Hercules' namesake city.
Now, everything is ruin, overwhelmed by fire, ash and grief.
    Even the almighty gods regret they were allowed to do this.

IV, 48

You love it rammed up your ass, really hard, Papylus.
    Afterwards you weep. Over what? As if you never wanted
what you wanted, penitent for that obscene itch? But
    maybe you're just sobbing because that rod's gone soft.

Book IV, 50

Why do you keep calling me old, Thais. No man's
an old man, Thais, pronging a mouth.

Sp. 11.

Praestitit exhibitus tota tibi, Caessar, harena
    quae non promisit proelia rhinoceros.
o quam terribilis exarsit pronus in iras!
    quantus erat taurus, cui pila taurus erat!

Sp. 12.

Laeserat ingrato leo perfidus ore magistrum,
    ausua tam notas contemerare manus;
sed dignas tanto persolvit crimine poenas,
    et qui non tulerat verbera, tela tulit.
quos decet esse hominum tali sub principe mores,
    qui iubet ingenium mitius esse feris!

Sp. 13.

Praeceps sanguinea dum se rotat ursus harena,
    implicitam visco perdidit ille fugam,
splendida iam tecto cessent venabula ferre,
    nec volet excussa lancea torta manu;
deprendat vacuo venator in aëre praedam,
    si captare feras aucupis arte placet.

Sp. 11.

The rhinoceros pacing, Caesar, circling the arena,
    delivered even more of a fight than promised!
Ah, how it lowered that terrible horn and charged in such a rage.
    One hell of a bull, who tossed that bull like a rag doll!

Sp. 12.

A treacherous lion gashed its trainer with its ungrateful
    mouth, daring to violate those familiar hands.
But that beast – who'd never felt the whip – quickly paid
    the price of its crime when it felt cold iron.
How else should men behave under a *princeps* like ours,
    who tells us to tame our animal nature?

Sp. 13.

While the bear was rolling, head over heels, he got
    mired – no more able to escape the blood soaked sand
than a pigeon stuck in birdlime. Sheathe your shining spears,
    don't let the spinning lance fly from your hand.
Save them for hunting in the air; let the birdcatcher's
    wiles – if you will – snare the wild animals.

BOOK V

Saturnalia 89 C.E.

V, 24

Hermes Martia saeculi voluptas.
Hermes omnibus eruditus armis,
Hermes et gladiator et magister,
Hermes turbo sui tremoque ludi,
Hermes, quem timet Helius, sed unum,
Hermes, cui cadit Advolans, sed uni,
Hermes vincere nec ferire doctus,
Hermes suppositicius sibi ipse,
Hermes divitiae locariorum,
Hermes cura laborque ludiarum,
Hermes belligera superbus hasta,
Hermes auquoreo minax tridente,
Hermes casside languida timendus,
Hermes gloria Martis universi,
Hermes omnia solus et ter unus.

V, 34

Hanc tibi, Fronto, pater, genetrix Flaccilla, puellam
    oscula commendo deliciasque meas,
parvula ne nigras horrescat Erotion umbras
    oraque Tartarei prodigiosa canis.
impletura fuit sextae modo frigora brumae,
    vixisset totidem ni minus illa dies.
inter iam veteres ludat lasciva patronos
    et nomen blaeso garriat ore meum.
mollia non rigidus caespes tegat ossa, nec illi,
    terra, gravis fueris: non fuit illa tibi.

V, 24

Hermes, sweetest battler of the era
Hermes, master of every weapon
Hermes, gladiator and manager too
Hermes, whirlwind and earthquake of the games
Hermes, who terrifies fearless Helius
Hermes, who toppled unconquerable Advolans
Hermes, crafty enough to win without killing
Hermes, who's his own reliever
Hermes, pure money at the gate
Hermes, heart throb and despair of gladiator girls
Hermes, of the proud thrusting spear
Hermes, perilous with the fisherman's trident
Hermes, grim behind the languid face plate
Hermes, glorious universal warrior
Hermes, all three in one, and one of a kind.

V, 34

Father Fronto, mother Flaccilla, protect this child
    who was my lips' delight. Don't let the darkness
and the snapping mouths of Tartarus' monstrous
    hound panic Erotion's shivering little shade.
She almost survived her sixth chilly winter.
    She lived just that many days too few.
Let her play and work her mischief on you, old
    guardians, and chatter away and garble my name.
Soft grass gently cover these gentle bones. Please
    earth, rest as lightly on her as she scampered over you.

V, 37

Puella senibus voce dulcior cycnis,
agna Galaesi mollior Phalantini,
concha Lucrini delicatior stagni,
cui nec lapillos praeferas Erythraeos
nec modo politum pecudis Indicae dentem
nivesque primas liliumque non tactum;
quae crine vicit Baetici gregis vellus
Rhenique nodos aureamque nitelam;
fragravit ore quod rosarium Paesti,
quod Atticarum prima mella cerarum,
quod sucinorum rapta de manu gleba;
cui comparatus indecens erat pavo,
inamabilis sciurus et frequens phoenix:

adhuc recenti tepet Erotion busto,
quam pessimorum lex amara fatorum
sexta peregit hieme, nec tamen tota,
nostros amores gaudiumque lususque.
et esse tristem me meus vetat Paetus,
pectusque pulsans pariter et comam vellens:
"deflere non te vernulae pudet mortem?
ego coniungen" inquit "extuli et tamen vivo,
notam, superbam, nobilem, locupletem."
quid esse nostro fortius potest Paeto?
ducentiens accepit et tamen vivit.

V, 46

Basia dum nolo nisi quae luctantia carpsi,
   et placet ira mihi plus tua quam facies,
ut te saepe rogem, caedo, Diadumene, saepe:
   consequor hoc, ut me nec timeas nec ames.

V, 37

A child with a voice as sweet as the fabled swan's,
gentler than a Galician lamb, delicate as a Lake Lucrine
oyster shell. Who you wouldn't trade for Red Sea pearls
or polished Indian ivory. A lily shimmering in new snow.
Her hair glowed like golden Baetic fleece, like German
curls, like a hazel dormouse. A girl whose soft breath
was as fragrant as damask roses, or Attic honey
fresh from the comb, or amber warmed in the hand.
Next to her, peacocks were crude, tiny squirrels
unlovable and the Phoenix nothing much.

Now Erotion lies still warm in the grave. The bitter
edict of brutal fate took her before even completing her
sixth winter. Our love and delight, my merry playmate.
And Paetus, my friend, forbids me to weep, beats his
own breast and tousles his hair: "Aren't you ashamed
to lose it over the death of a little house slave" he says.
"I buried my wife – but I got on with my life. And she
was a socialite from the old nobility, proud and wealthy
in her own right." Who can set a braver example than our
Paetus? He collects twenty million and gets on with his life.

V, 46

I only want those kisses I force out of you. Diadumenus.
    Your anger enchants me even more than your looks.
More often than not, I slap you to caress you. And
    then, you neither fear me, nor, sadly, love me.

V, 64

Sextantes, Calliste, duos infunde Falerni,
    tu super aestiuas, Alcime, solve nives;
pinguescat nimio madidus mihi crinis amomo
    lassenturque rosis tempora sutilibus.
Tam vicina iubent non vivere Mausolea,
    cum doceant ipsos posse perire deos.

V, 64

Callistus pour a quadruple Falernian measure.
   And you, Alcimus, add some summer snowmelt.
Oil my hair with fragrant amber and wreathe
   roses around my crown. The Imperial *Mausolea*,
across the way, command us to live despite it
   all, while teaching us even gods can die.

Sp. 14.

Inter Caesareae discrimina saeva Dianae
   fixisset gravidam cum levis hasta suem,
exiluit partus miserae de vulnerae matris
   o Lucina ferox, hoc peperisse fuit?
pluribus illa mori voluisset saucia telis,
   omnibus et natis triste pateret iter.
quis negat esse satum materno funere Bacchum?
   sic genitum numen credite: nata fera est.

*Sp.*15.

Icta gravi telo confossaque vulnere mater
   sus pariter vitam perdidit atque dedit.
o quam certa fuit librato dextera ferro!
   hanc ego Lucinae credo fuisse manum.
experta est numen moriens utriusque Dianae,
   quaque soluta parens quaque perempta fera est.

Sp. 16.

Sus fera iam gravior maturi pignora ventris
   emisit fetum, vulnere facta parens;
nec iacuit partus, sed matre cadente cucurrit.
   o quantum est subitis casibus ingenium!

Sp. 14.

In the midst of the savage forays of Caesar's sacred hunt,
Diana – a nimble spear point slit a heavily pregnant sow.
Then, one of her litter plopped out of its poor mother's wound.

O, Diana Lucina: fierce huntress, holy midwife. Which of your aspects
attended this delivery? Because the sow prayed to be finished off, hoping
more javelins might open a sad pathway for the rest of her brood.

And who, now, can deny that Bacchus entered life by
way of his mother's death? Because you have to believe
in divinity, when animals are born like this.

Sp.15.

The heavy spear rammed and pierced the mother sow
    and from that wound she, simultaneously, lost and gave life.
Oh how dexterous, precise and restrained was the hand
    that guided the iron tip. Of course, it had to be Lucina's hand.
In dying, the sow experienced the divinity of both
    Dianas: The grace of one, delivered the parent.
The other, gracefully dispatched the animal.

Sp. 16.

A wild sow, already heavy and ripe with pregnant promise,
    gave up her litter and became a parent through her wound.
The piglets didn't just lay there. Even as their mother was falling,
    they scampered away. Ah, how emergency breeds precocity!

BOOK VI
Summer / Autumn 90 c.e.

VI, 2

Lusus erat sacrae conubia taedae,
  lusus et immeritos exsecuisse mares.
Utraque tu prohibes, Caesar, populisque futuris
  succurris, nasci quos sine fraude iubes.
Nec spado iam nec moechus erit te praeside quisquam:
  at prius—o mores—et spado moechus erat.

VI, 4

Censor maxime principumque princeps,
cum tot iam tibi debeat triumphos,
tot nascentia templa, tot renata,
tot spectacula, tot deos, tot urbes,
plus debet tibi Roma quod pudica est.

VI, 23

Stare iubes semper nostrum tibi, Lesbia, penem:
  crede mihi, non est mentula quod digitus.
Tu licet et manibus blandis et vocibus instes,
  te contra facies imperiosa tua est.

VI, 2

The rites of sacred wedlock meant nothing; it was
    nothing to castrate innocent boys. You said "no
more", Caesar, and decreed the birth of a new,
    forthright generation. Under your watchful eyes,
we'll no longer see eunuchs or adulterers. Before
    – *o mores* – we even had eunuch adulterers.

VI, 4

Magnificent *Censor*, sovereign Sovereign, as
much as she owes you for so many triumphs,
so many new temples, so much renewal, so
many shows, and gods, and cities, Rome
owes you even more for her chastity.

VI, 23

"Do your duty", you like to command my weenie.
    Take it from me, Lesbia, a prick can't salute like
a finger. Coax all you like with your hands and that
    insistent voice. Your imperious mug decrees defeat.

VI, 34

Basia da nobis, Diadumene, pressa. "Quot?" inquis.
    Oceani fluctus me numerare iubes
et maris Aegaei sparsas per litora conchas
    et quae Cecropio monte uagantur apes,
quaeque sonant pleno vocesque manusque theatro
    cum populus subiti Caesaris ora videt.
Nolo quot arguto dedit exorata Catullo
    Lesbia: pauca cupit qui numerare potest.

VI, 39

Pater ex Marulla, Cinna, factus es septem
non liberorum: namque nec tuus quisquam
nec est amici filiusue vicini,
sed in grabatis tegetibusque concepti
materna produnt capitibus suis furta.

Hic qui retorto crine Maurus incedit
subolem fatetur esse se coci Santrae;
at ille sima nare, turgidis labris
ipsa est imago Pannychi palaestritae.
Pistores esse tertium quis ignorat,
quicumque lippum novit et videt Damam?

Quartus cinaeda fronte, candido voltu
ex concubino natus est tibi Lygdo:
percide, si vis, filium: nefas non est.
Hunc vero acuto capite et auribus longis,
quae sic moventur ut solent asellorum,

quis morionis filium negat Cyrtae?
Duae sorores, illa nigra et haec rufa,
Croti choraulae uilicique sunt Carpi.
Iam Niobidarum grex tibi foret plenus
si spado Coresus Dindymusque non esset.

VI, 34

Overwhelm me with kisses, Diadumenus, don't ask
   how many. Can you count the ocean waves, the sea
shells on the Aegean shore, the buzzing Attic honeybees?
   Or tally the rustle and applause as the audience
catches sight of Caesar entering the crowded theater?
   I don't want just the thousands Lesbia lavished when
she finally gave in to cunning Catullus. If what I want
   had any limits, it wouldn't be enough for me.

VI, 39

Marulla's made you the proud father of seven.
Well, not really Cinna. Because not a one of them
is yours, or even your elegant friends' or neighbors'.
Conceived on blankets or whatever cot was handy,
their faces betray their mother's sly, vulgar romps.

This one, trooping in like a kinky haired Moor: He's
obviously the offspring of Santra the cook. And
that flat nosed, liver lip is the spitting image of
Pannychus the wrestling coach. Can anyone
look into the third one's rheumy eyes and not see

Dama the baker's familiar drip. The fourth's pouty looks
and pansy airs were a gift from your favorite butt pal,
Lygdus. Go ahead and fuck this son, no crime there.
And here, with the pointy head and long ears he wiggles
like an ass, you can't deny, is Cyrtus the moron's boy.

Then we have two sisters, one a negress, the other
a red head, sired respectively, by Crotus the flute
player and your slave overseer, Carpus. Ah, you
might even have had as many as weeping Niobe,
if Coresus and Dindymus weren't eunuchs.

VI, 40

Femina praeferri potuit tibi nulla, Lycori:
  praeferri Glycera femina nulla potest
haec erit hoc quod tu: tu non potes esse quod haec est.
  tempora quid faciunt! hanc volo, te volui.

VI, 45

Lusistis, satis est: lascivi nubite cunni:
  permissa est vobis non nisi casta Venus.
Haec est casta Venus? Nubit Laetoria Lygdo:
  turpius uxor erit quam modo moecha fuit.

VI, 60

Laudat, amat, cantat nostros mea Roma libellos,
  meque sinus omnes, me manus omnis habet.
ecce rubet quidam, pallet, stupet, oscitat, odit.
  hoc volo; nunc nobis carmina nostra placent.

VI, 90

Moechum Gellia non habet nisi unum.
turpe est hoc magis: uxor est duorum.

VI, 40

I never cared more for a woman than you, Lycoris,
  but Glycera is the only woman I care about.
She's become you. You can't be her. Time
  does that. I want her. I wanted you.

VI, 45

Ladies, you've frolicked to your hearts' content, get your
  wild cunts married. Only proper love's allowed now.
Ah, proper love: Laetoria's marrying Lygdus? That
  shameless slut is soon to be a truly shameless matron.

VI, 60

My Rome applauds, loves, recites our little books.
  I get to sit on every lap, be held in every hand.
Watch them blush, pale, gasp, yawn, gag. Just
  what I wanted: now our poetry makes us smile.

VI, 90

Gellia has a lover, but just that one and only.
Adultery is bad enough, but this is bigamy.

Sp, 17.

Summa tuae, Meleagre, fuit quae gloria famae
    quanta est Corpophori portio, fusus aper!
ille et praecipiti venabula conditit urso,
    primus in Arctoi qui fuet axe poli,
stravit et ignota spectandum mole leonem,
    Herculeas potuit qui decuisse manus,
et volucrem longo porrexit vulnere pardum
    ....
....
    praemia cum laudem ferret, at hic pateram.

Sp. 18.

Raptus abit media quod ad aethera taurus harena.
    non fuit hoc artis, sed pietatis opus.

Sp. 19.

Vexerat Europen fraterna per aequora taurus:
    et nunc Alciden taurus in astra tulit.
Caesaris atque Iovis confer nunc, Fama, iuvencos:
    par onus et tulerint, altius iste tulit.

Sp, 17.

You know, Meleager, the sum total of all your fame and glory,
    is just of fraction of Corpophorus': Gettng rid of a boar?
Sure, but he also buried his spear in a huge charging bear
    who once ruled the arctic. Then brought down
a never before witnessed monster of a lion, one
    worthy of Hercules' hands. Then stretched out
a running leopard with his flying javelin....

....

....

... (?) has earned due praise, the other, a libation.

Sp. 18.

The marvel of the bull snatched up from the middle of the arena
    into the firmament, wasn't the stagecraft, but its submission.

Sp. 19.

Disguised as a bull, He ferried his Europa across his brother's sea:
    Now, a bull has taken our Little Hercules right up into the stars.
So the wags are comparing Jove's and Caesar's young bulls – they
    carried much the same weight, but which one sailed it further?...

BOOK VII

Saturnalia 92 c.e.

VII, 14

Accidit infandum nostrae scelus, Aule, puellae;
    amisit lusus deliciasque suas:
non quales teneri ploravit amica Catulli
    Lesbia, nequitiis passeris orba sui,
vel Stellae cantata meo quas flevit Ianthis,
    cuius in Elysio nigra columba volat:
lux mea non capitur nugis neque moribus istis
    nec dominae pectus talia damna movent:
bis senos puerum numerantem perdidit annos,
    mentula cui nondum sesquipedalis erat.

VII, 21

Haec est illa dies, magni quae conscia partus
    Lucanum populus et tibi, Polla, dedit.
heu! Nero crudelis nullaque invisior umbra,
    debuit hoc saltem non licuisse tibi.

VII, 89

I, felix rosa, mollibusque sertis
nostri cinge comas Apollinaris.
Quas tu nectere candidas, sed olim,
sic te semper amet Venus, memento.

VII, 14

Ah, Aulus, what happened to my girl is obscene.
  Death robbed her of her adorable pet. Not
the kind fragile Catullus' soul mate mourned;
  Lesbia's forlorn naughty sparrow. Or even
the tragic turtle dove, cooing in Elysium now, that
  moved my Ianthis to tears and Stella to poetry.
The light of my life isn't enthralled by such niceties.
  Genteel disasters don't stir my mistress's heart.
She lost a slave, barely twice six years old, whose
  dick was already approaching eighteen inches.

VII, 21

Today we commemorate a great birthday, the day
  that gave Lucan to humanity, and to you, Polla.
Damn it, vicious Nero, for no ghost more despised, this
  victim, at least, you shouldn't have been allowed.

VII, 89

Wreathe, blessed rose, all your sweet delicacy
around our Apollinaris' hair. Now and in that
distant hour when it's silver, may Venus
always love you, and linger.

Generally identified as Domitius Apollinaris, a senator and, in 97, a consul. An intimate
friend and respected sounding board for Martial's verse. This poem may commemorate
a wedding or anniversary, or be an occasional piece for a birthday celebration.

VII, 91

De nostro, facunde, tibi, Iuvenalis, agello
  Saturnalicias mittimus, ecce, nuces.
Cetera lascivis donavit poma puellis
  mentula custodis luxuriosa dei.

VII, 91

Here, for Saturnalia, silver-tongued Juvenal, as you can
    see, are nuts from our little orchard. Alas, the Priapus
who guards the place with his big stiff prick, gave all
    the apples away to dulcet little country sluts.

Sp. 20.

Quod pius et supplex elephas te, Caesar, adorat
   hic modo qui tauro tam metuendos erat
non facit hoc iussus, nulloque docente magistro:
   crede mihi, nostrum sentit et ille deum.

Sp. 21.

Lambere securi dextram consueta magistri
   tigris, ab Hyrcano gloria rara iugo,
saeva ferum rabido laceravit dente leonem:
   res nova, non ullis cognita temporibus.
ausa est tale nihil, silvis dum vixit in altis:
   postquam inter nos est, plus feritatis habet.

Sp. 22.

Qui modo per totam flammis stimulatus harenam
   sustulerat raptas taurus in astra pilas,
occubuit tandem cornuto adore petitus,
   dum facilem tolli sic elephanta putat.

Sp. 23.

Cum peteret pars haec Myrinum, pars illa Triumphum,
   promisit pariter Caesar utraque manu.
non potuit melius litem finire iocosam
   o dulce invicti principis ingenium!

Sp. 20.

That same elephant, who just now was so brutal to
   a bull, piously kneels and reveres you, Caesar.
Believe me, no trainer coached or commanded this.
   He just senses the presence of our god.

Sp. 21.

A tigress, who likes to come lick the hand of her
   relaxing trainer, a rare glory from the Hyrcanian
hills – savagely tore a wild lion apart with her raging teeth:
   Something new, completely unknown before our time.
She dared no such thing while she lived in the high forest.
   Now, she's one of us, and more ferocious.

Sp. 22.

The way a seething bull, prodded around the arena by burning
   goads, tosses one taunting rag dummy after another to the stars.
How it's finished off by fervid tusks; finally enraged enough to imagine
   an elephant might be tossed as easily.

Sp. 23.

Half the crowd shouted for Myrinus, the other half, Triumphus.
   Caesar just threw up both hands – and that released them both!
The only good ending possible to a silly dispute.
   Oh, the sweet spontaneity of an infallible ruler…

BOOK VIII
Late 93 / early 94 C.E.

VIII, 30

Qui nunc Caesarae lusus spectatur harenae,
    temporibus Bruti gloria summa fuit.
aspicis ut teneat flammas poenaque fruatur
    fortis et attonito regnet in igne manus!
ipse sui spectator adest et nobile dextrae
    funus amat: totis pascitur illa sacris.
quod nisi rapta foret nolenti poena, parabat
    saevior in lassos ira sinestra focos.
scire piget post tale decus quid fecerit ante:
    quam vidi satis hanc est mihi nosse manum.

VIII, 35

Cum sitis similes paresque vita,
uxor pessima, pessimus maritus,
miror non bene convenere vobis.

VIII, 30

That pinnacle of glory from old Brutus' age is now
   a diversion to enjoy in Caesar's Arena. See how
his hand caresses the flame and regally revels in
   its, almost fascinating, punishment. He's his own
spectator now, in love with the nobility of his right hand's
   funeral. His hand feasts on the sacrificial pyre.
If they hadn't yanked him away, he might even have
   shoved his left hand into the dying brazier. After such
a fine show, I don't care to know what he did to earn this.
   It's enough to remember that hand as I watched it.

(ref. I, 21 A reenactment of the Mucius Scaevola legend)

VIII, 35

The two of you lead such similar lives,
a no-good husband, and a no-good wife.
I'm amazed you're so incompatible.

VIII, 44

Titulle, moneo, vive: semper hoc serum est;
sub paedagogo coeperis licet, serum est.
at tu, miser Titulle, nec senex vivis,
sed omne limen conteris salutator
et mane sudas urbis osculis udus.

foroque triplici sparsus ante equos omnes
aedemque Martis et colloson Augusti
curris per omnes tertiasque quintasque.
rape, congere, aufer, posside: relinquendum est.
superba densis arca palleat nummis,

centum explicentur paginae Kalendarum,
iurabit heres te nihil reliquisse,
supraque pluteum te iacente vel saxum,
fartus papyro dum tibi torus crescit,
flentis superbus basiabit eunuchos;

tuoque tristis filius, velis nolis,
cum concubino nocte dormiet prima.

VIII, 51

Formosam sane, sed caecus diligit Asper.
   plus ergo, ut res est, quam videt Asper amat.

VIII, 44

Take my advice, Titullus, start living: it's always
past time for that. Even when you were a schoolboy,
it was past time. But old as you are, poor Titullus,
you don't even try to live. Polishing every threshold
making your patron calls. Out early, sweating and trading

wet kisses with half the City. Hitting all three Forums,
mud-spattered at the statues on horseback, the Temple
of Mars and Augustus' Colossus. You're in a constant
rush every hour of the day. Grab, collect, finagle,
hoard all you can: You'll still lose it all when you die.

Your proud strongbox is packed with pale coins,
but your heir will swear you left nothing to cover
the notes coming due. While you're laid out on a plank
or stone and they're stuffing the pyre with papyrus,
he'll be arrogantly kissing your weeping eunuchs.

And that sad son, like it or not, will sleep
with the boy you loved best, that very night

VIII, 51

Asper's picked a flawless beauty, but Asper's blind. Proof again,
    from a man in love: Beauty's so much more than meets the eye.

Sp. 24.

Quidquid in Orpheo Rhodope spectasse theatro
    dicitur, exhibuit, Caesar, harena tibi.
Repserunt scopuli mirandaque silva curcurrit
    quale fuisse nemus creditur Hesperidum
adfuit inmixtum pecori genus omne ferarum,
    et supra vatem multa pependit avis,
ipse sed ingrato iacuit laceratus ab urso.
    haec tantum res est facta 'par historian'.

Sp. 25.

Orphea quod subito tellus emisit hiatu
    ursam invasuram, venit ab Eurydice.

Sp. 26.

Sollicitant pavidi dum rhinocerota magistri
    seque diu magnae colligit ira ferae,
desperabantur promissi proelia Martis;
    sed tandem rediit cognitus ante furor.
namque gravem cornu gemino sic extulit ursum,
    iactat ut impositas taurus in astra pilas.

(Norica quam certo venabula derigit ictu
    fortis adhuc teneri dextera Carpophori!)*

ille tulit geminos facile cervice iuvencos,
    illi cessit atrox bubalus atque vison:
hunc leo cum fugere, praeceps in tela cucurrit
    i nunc et lentas corripe, turba, moras!

Sp. 24.

Everything the stage can depict about Orpheus on the slopes
    of Rhodope – Caesar – the arena sands outdo for you.
Rocky cliffs slowly appear, then an ancient forest springs
    miraculously alive, a veritable garden of Hesperides.
All the wild animals and cattle mingle together, and fluttering
    over the poet's head, a multitude of singing birds.
But then the ingrate bear rips him to shreds.
    Just that one, small deviation from the script.

Sp. 25.

The earth suddenly opened and a bear emerged
    to work over Orpheus. Eurydice sent her.

Sp. 26.

The nervous handlers kept goading the rhinoceros. The
    lumbering beast seemed to take forever to gather
its rage. And the fickle crowd gave up on the touted battles.
    But finally, that fury we remembered – when
its double horns hoisted the huge bear as easily as
    a bull tosses a helpless rag dummy to the stars.

Then how nicely Carpophorus' clever hand aimed
    his razor sharp darts' maddening cuts.

It went for a pair of young bulls with its twisting neck,
    A fierce buffalo and bison backed off. And a panicked lion
retreated headlong back into the prodding spears.
Okay you rabble, go gripe now about those tedious delays…

(* There's disagreement about whether the two lines about Corpophorus may be
displaced from another, unknown, poem. My reading is a conjecture of what M. might
be referring to.)

BOOK IX
Late 94 / early 95 C.E.

IX 5

Tibi, summe Rheni domitor et parens orbis,
pudice princeps, gratias agunt urbes:
populos habebunt; parere iam scelus non est.
non puer avari sectus arte mangonis
virilitatis damna maeret ereptae,
nec quam superbus conputet stipem leno
dat prostituto misera mater infanti.
Qui nec cubili fuerat ante te quondam,
pudor esse per te coepit et lupanari.

IX, 32

Hanc volo quae facilis, quae palliolata vagatur.
 hanc volo quae puero iam dedit ante meo.
hanc volo quam redimit totam denarius alter,
 hanc volo quae pariter sufficit una tribus.
poscentem nummos et grandia verba sonantem
 possideat crassae mentula Burdigalae.

IX, 63

Ad cenam invitant omnes te, Phoebe, cinaedi.
 mentula quem pascit, non, puto, purus homo est.

IX 5

Supreme Conqueror of the Rhine. Father of the World,
and *Princeps* of Wholesomeness: the cities all thank you.
Populations can increase again, parenting no longer means
crime. Boys, snipped by the slave dealers' greedy guiles
won't have to sob over their ruined manhood. Imperious
pimps can stop gauging the minimum pittance a heartsick
mother will take for her prostituted toddler. Decency,
which before you, barely survived in the nuptial bed,
begins, with your decree, to flourish even in the brothel.

IX, 32

I want a girl who's easy, who walks around in a shortie.
    One who'll have my boy while I do. Who laughs
and says sure to everything for a few denarii.
    A girl who kind of likes a three way. Those hustlers
    with price lists they tout in tempting detail;
save them for some provincial's unimaginative prick.

IX, 63

They all like having you over for dinner, Phoebus, the pretty
    boys. But dick, I don't think, is a very healthy meal.

IX, 67

Lascivam tota possidi nocte puellam,
   cuius nequitias vincere nemo potest.
fessus mille modis illud puerile poposci:
   ante preces totum primaque verba dedit.
improbius quiddam ridensque rubensque rogavi:
   pollicita est nulla luxuriosa mora.
sed mihi pura fuit; tibi non erit, Aeschyle, si vis
   accipere hoc munus condicione mala

IX, 67

I spent the whole night with a lascivious girl whose itch had
    no limits. We did it a thousand ways, and when I needed
something to refresh me, I wondered if she'd play the boy.
    Before I could even say it, she turned over. Laughing
and blushing, I asked what other shameless pleasures she knew.
    Then she took me places I'd never imagined. To me, she
was pure innocence. But she wouldn't be for you Aeschylus.
    Because you only know how to play by your own sick rules.

Sp. 27.

Si quis ades longis serus spectator ab oris,
    cui lux prima sacri muneris ista fuit,
ne te decipiat ratibus navalis Enyo
    et par unda fretis: hic modo terra fuit.
non credis? speeta, dum lassant aequora Martem:
    parva mora est, dices "hic modo pontus erat."

Sp. 28.

Quod nocturna tibi, Leandrem pepercerit unda,
    desine mirari; Cesaris unda fuit.

Sp. 29.

Cum peteret dulces audax Leandros amores
    et fessus tumidis iam premeretur aquis,
sic miser instantes affatus dicitur undas:
    "parcite dum propero, mergite dum redeo".

Sp. 27.

If you're a spectator just arrived from far off shores,
    this morning's sacred presentation, your first show;
don't let bloody Enyo's naval slaughter fool you – the boats,
    the waves, just like a bay. Just a bit ago, this was all
dry land. You don't believe? Just watch until her
    waters weary even Mars. In a little while, you'll
be saying, "Here, just a bit ago, was a sea."

Sp. 28.

Of course, the swirling night waters spared
    you, Leander. They were Caesar's waters.

(Recent archeological studies suggest that the Roman Colosseum could be mechanically
flooded to a depth of just some five feet.)

Sp. 29.

While Leander was heedlessly pursuing his sweet love,
    and already yielding to the pressure of the swelling flow,
the poor guy is said to have urgently addressed the waves:
    "Just let me get there. You can drown me after, on the ebb tide."

Sp. 30.

Lusit Nereidum docilis chorus aequore toto
   et vario faciles ordine pinxit aquas
fuscina dente minax recto fuit, ancora curvo:
   credidimus remum credidimusque ratem,
et gratum nautis sidus fulgere Laconum
   lataque perspicuo vela tumere sinu.
quis tantas liquidis artes invenit in undis?
   aut docuit lusus hos Thetis aut didcit.

Sp. 30.

A disciplined chorus of Nereids frolics on the waters
    painting the still surface with a series of pantomimes.
We think we see an oar, and then we see – a boat. Neptune's
    fearsome trident teeth poke up above a graceful anchor.
Castor and Pollux in the stars shine down their sailors'
    blessing, and a broad, billowing sail proudly unfurls.
Who contrived such a wonderfully flowing aquatic show?
    Is Thetis coaching, or learning from them?

BOOK X

Saturnalia 95, revised and reisssued mid-98 after Domitian's assassination

X, 20

Nec doctum satis et parum severum,
sed non rusticulum tamen libellum
facundo mea Plinio Thalia
i perfer: brevis est labor peractae
altum vincere tramitem Suburae.

Illic Orphea protinus videbis
udi vertice lubricum theatri
mirantisque feras avemque regis,
raptum quae Phryga pertulit Tonanti;
illic parva tui domus Pedonis

caelata est aquilae minore pinna.
Sed ne tempore non tuo disertam
pulses ebria ianuam, videto:
Totos dat tetricae dies Minervae,
dum centum studet auribus virorum

hoc quod saecula posterique possint
Arpinis quoque conparare chartis.
Seras tutior ibis ad lucernas:
haec hora est tua, cum furit Lyaeus,
cum regnat rosa, cum madent capilli:
tunc me vel rigidi legant Catones

X, 20

Not that it's scholarly, or even serious – but
Thalia, my merry muse, please carry this,
not uncouth, small book to eloquent Pliny.
You'll have to navigate, then climb the steep
path out of, teeming Suburra. But after that:

an easy stroll. Once there you'll see sprinkled
Orpheus, presiding over his fountain audience
of enchanted beasts and the regal bird that
snatched up Ganymede for thunderous Jove.
And you'll find Pedo's old cottage from Ovid's

time preserved like a shrine, engraved with
its own little eagle. But don't get tipsy and
eager and rap on the counselor's door at a time
that's not for you. He spends every daylight
minute agonizing over those luminous

court orations that posterity will preserve
and rank with Cicero's. Play it safe and wait
until the evening lamps are lit. That's your
special hour; when the wine is poured, when
the rose is queen, when hair's shaken loose.
Then, even grumpy old Catos recite me.

X, 25

In matutina nuper spectatus harena
   Mucius, inposuit qui sua, membra focis,
si patiens durusque tibi fortisque videtur,
   Adberitanae pectora plebis habes.
nam cum dicatur tunica praesente molesta
   "Ure manum," plus est dicere "Non facio."

X, 47

Vitam quae faciant beatiorem,
iucundissime Martialis, haec sunt:
res non parta labore, sed relicta;
non ingratus ager, focus perrenis;
lis numquam, toga rara, mens quieta;
vires ingenuae, salubre corpus;
prudens simplicitas, pares amici;
convictus facilis, sine arte mensa;
nox non ebria, sed solura curis;
non tristis torus et tamen pudicus;
somnus qui faciat breves tenebras:
quod sis esse velis nihilque malis;
summum nec metuas diem nec optes.

X, 61

Hic festinata requiescit Erotion umbra,
   crimine quam fati sexta peremit hiems.
quisquis eris nostri post me regnator agelli,
   Manibus exiguis annua iusta dato:
sic lare perpetuo, sic turba sospite solus
   flebilis in terra sit lapis iste tua.

X, 25

If you thought that "Mucius" you watched
    the other morning in the Arena, holding
his hand in the flames, was a picture of endurance,
    courage and strength, you're a rube from the sticks.
When they show you the *tunica molesta*, then say
    "Burn your hand", it's really tough to say "I won't".

(*ref. VIII, 30*)

X, 47

What makes life happy, gracious cousin Martial?
A little money in the family, some not unthankful
farmland, and a hearth with plenty of firewood.
Lawsuits? Never. Business you have to dress
for? Hardly ever. But a peaceful mind, in
a gentleman's, unstrained body. Savvy
simplicity and unpretentious friends.
Relaxed dinners, easy conversation. Nights,
by no means drunken, but really mellow.
Until you tumble into a wise, gentle bed.
Sleep that makes the dark hours short. And
wanting to be nothing more than who you are,
not craving, not dreading, the end of it all.

X, 61

Here rests Erotion's hurried shade, robbed
    of life by fate and her sixth winter. Whoever
owns this little plot after me, make an offering
    to her small ghost each year. Then, may your
household endure, safe and untroubled.
    Let this stone be the only sorrow on your land.

X, 63

Marmora parva quidem sed non cessura, viator,
  Mausoli saxis pyramidumque legis.
bis mea Romano spectata est vita Tarento
  et nihil extremos perdidit ante rogos:
quinque dedit pueros, totidem mihi Iuno puellas,
  cluserunt omnes lumina nostra manus.
contigit et thalami mihi gloria rara fuitque
  una pudicitae mentula nota meae.

X, 72

Frustra, Blanditiae, venitis ad me
attritis miserabiles labellis:
dicturus dominum deumque non sum.
iam non est locus hac in urbe vobis;
ad Parthos procul ite pilleatos
et turpes humilesque supplicesque
pictorum sola basiate regum.
non est hic dominus, sed imperator,
sed iustissimus omnium senator,
per quem de Stygia domo reducto est
siccis rustica Veritas capillis.
hoc sub principe, si sapis, caveto
verbis, Roma, prioribus loquaris.

X, 63

This gravestone you're reading may be small,
    traveler, but cedes nothing to any mausoleum or
pyramid. I attended not one, but two Saecular
    Games, sixty four years apart, and never lost a step
until my dying day. Juno gave me five boys and as
    many girls, and every one of their hands
closed my eyes. My marriage was a glory to
    behold, and I was faithful to just that one prick.

X, 72

Now my flatteries are a waste of time,
my shameless grovelling lips no longer
mouth out "lord and god". There's no
more place for that in the City. Go
far, far away to turbaned Persia, if you
want to humiliate and abase yourself and
kneel to kiss the feet of self styled kings.
There's no *Dominus* here now, but a real *Imperator*,
the most upright of all senators bringing dry,
homespun truth back from the dead.
Under this *princeps,* Rome, you'd be wise to
avoid talking the way you used to talk.

Sp. 31.

Cum traheret Priscus, traheret certamina Verus,
  esset et aequalis Mars utriusque diu,
missio saepe viris magno clamore petita est;
  sed Caesar legi parvit ipsae suae
(lex erat ad digitum posita concurrere palma):
  quod licuit , lances donaque saepe dedit.
inventus tamen est finis discriminus aequi:
  pugnavere pares, succubuere pares.
misit utrique rudes et palmas Caesar utrique.
  hoc pretium virtus ingeniosa tulit.
contigit hoc nullo nisi te sub principe, Caesar:
  cum duo pugnarent, victor uterque fuit.

Sp. 32.

Saecula Carpophorum, Caesar, si prisca tulissent,
  non amarathon cum barbara terra fera,
non Marathon taurum, Nemee frondosa leonem,
  Arcus Maenaleum non timuisset aprum.
hoc armante manus Hydrae mors una fuisset,
  huic percussa foret tota Chimaera semel.
igniferos possit sine Colchide iungere tauros,
  possit utramque feram vincere Pasiphaes.
si vetus aequorei revocetur fabula monstri,
  Hesionen solvet solus et Andromedan.
Hercules laudis numeretur gloriae, plus est
  bis denas pariter perdomuisse feras.

Sp. 31.

Priscus desperately played for time, Verus struggled to hold
    on too. Neither could get the better of their mortal
combat. The awed crowd kept chanting for the magnificent,
    exhausted men's reprieve. But Caesar was bound by
the letter of his own law. (The rules were clear, there had to be
    a winner. Only a raised finger could stop the bout.)
Caesar did what he could to calm things with food and trinkets.
    Then, he found a way to end the crisis. They'd battled
to a brutal draw, now each was dead on his feet. Caesar gave
    them both, not just a reprieve – but each the *palma*
of victory and the *rudis* of liberty. It's never
    happened before, under any *princeps*, Caesar:
A pair who fought to the finish until both were victorious.

(A raised gladiator finger was the equivalent of "throwing in the towel".)

Sp. 32.

Ages ago, Caesar, when the uncvilized earth teemed
    with angry animals; if only they had Carpophorus, then.
Marathon wouldn't have feared the bull, nor leafy
    Nemea that lion, and the Arcadians needn't have fretted
over the Erymanthanian boar. Weapons in hand,
    he'd have whacked off all of Hydra's heads in one sweep,
and, with a single blow, smashed the entire Chimaera. He
    could have yoked the fire-breathing bulls without Medea's
black magic, and tamed both of Pasiphae's horrid creatures.
    And if you want to resurrect those old sea monster stories;
Hesione and Andromeda would need no other savior.
    Total up and praise every one of Hercules' glories. They
don't match "twice-ten killer beasts despatched in a day".

Sp. 33.

Concita veloces fugeret com damma Molossos
    et varia lentas necteret arte moras,
Caesaris ante pedes supplex similesque rogant
    constitit et praedam non tetigere canes
....
...haec intellecto principe dona tulit.
numen habet, Caesar: sacra est haec, sacra potestas.
    credite: mentiri non didicere ferae.

Sp. 34.

Augusti labor hic fuerat committere classes
    et freta navali sollicitare tuba.
Caesaris haec nostri pars est quota? vidit in undis
    et Thetis ignotas et Galatea feras;
vidit in aequoreo ferventes pulvere currus
    et domini Triton isse putavit equos:
dumque parat saevis ratibus fera proelia Nereus,
    horruit in liquidis ire pedestris aquis.
quidquid et in Circo spectatur et Amphitheatro,
    id dives, Caesar, praestitit unda tibi.
Fucines et tigri taceantur stagna Neronis:
    hanc norint unam saecula naumachiam.

Sp. 33.

The panicked little deer came bounding in flight
   from the vicious mastiffs. Looking for anything that
might impede the chase, she sought refuge
   in front of Caesar, falling as if in supplication.
The hunting pack stopped and didn't touch their prey…

   …by acknowledging her *princeps,* she won her reward.
Caesar's divinity is sacred, a sacred, numinous power.
   Believe me: Animals haven't learned to lie.

Sp. 34.

Augustus staged his elaborate naval engagements,
   whole fleets clashing, trumpets blaring.
They're just some fraction of our Caesar's show:
   Gaping at the waves, Thetis and Galatea see incongruous
animals. Triton, startled by horses tearing along the foaming
   sands, wonders if it was his master Neptune's chariot.
And Old Man Nereus, diagramming a battle of boats, is
   dumbstruck by wading infantry on the attack.
Everything ever seen in the Circus and Amphitheater,
   Caesar, your teeming waters eclipse… Forget Lake
Fucine and Nero's ruthless lagoon, this was
   naumachia for the centuries, truly one of a kind…

(*Naumachiae* were elaborate mock naval battles fought, in earnest, by convicts most of whom were not excpected to survive.)

BOOK XI
Saturnalia 96 c.e.

XI, 19

Quaeris cur nolim te ducere, Galla? diserta es.
   saepe soloescismum mentula nostra facit.

XI, 21

Lydia tam laxa est equitis quam culus aeni,
   quam celer arguto qui sonat aere trochus,
quam rota transmisso totiens inpacta petauro,
   quam vetus a crassa calceus udus aqua,
quam quae rara vagos expectant retia turdos,
   quam Pompeiano vela negata Noto,
quam quae de pthisico lapsa est armilla cinaedo,
   culcita Leuconico quam viduata suo,
quam veteres bracae Brittonis pauperis, et quam
   urpe Ravennatis guttur onocrotali.
Hanc in piscina dicor futuisse marina.
   Nescio; piscinam me futuisse puto.

XI, 25

Illa salax nimium naec paucis nota puellis
   stare Lino desit mentula. Lingua, cave.

XI, 30

Os male causidicis et dicis olere poetis,
   sed fellatori, Zoilem, peius olet.

XI, 19

Why won't I marry you, Galla? We're literati,
   we connect. But my cock speaks a coarser language.

XI, 21

Lydia, as spacious as the ass of a bronze statue's horse,
      as open as the tinkling hoops boys whip down the street,
or one of those wheels acrobats dive through. She's
      a comfy old shoe soaked in squishy rainwater. A wide
net set to snag stray robins. As vast as the canvas that blocks
      the summer wind at Pompey's Theater. Or an armlet
that's grown too big for a wheezing tubercular queen.
      A lambswool mattress whose stuffing has gone.
That grizzled British beggar's drooping britches.
      A Ravenna wharf pelican's gulping pouch.
Someone reminded me I fucked her in the seawater
      pool. I don't know, I think I fucked the sea.

XI, 25

That oversexed prick more than a few girls know so well,
   won't stand up for Linus. Uh oh tongue, your turn.

XI, 30

Lawyers and poets: They're real shit-mouths, you tell me.
   But, cocksuckers, Zoilus, have the worst breath of all.

XI, 46

Iam nisi per somnum non arrigis et tibi, Mevi,
   incipit in medios meiere verpa pedes,
truditur et digites pannucea mentula lassis
   nec levat extinctum sollicitata caput.
quid miseros frustra cunnos culosque lacessis?
   summa petas: illic mentula vivit anus.

XI, 66

Et delator es et calumniator,
et fraudator es et negotiator,
et fellator es et lanista. miror
quare non habeas, Vacerra, nummos.

XI, 87

Dives eras quondam: sed tunc pedico fuisti
   et tibi nulla des femina fuit.
nunc sectaris anus. o quantum cogit egestas!
   illa fututorem te, Charideme, facit.

XI, 46

It only awakens, now, in your sleep, Mevius. And
   when you piss in the middle of the night, your
knob just dribbles on your feet. You keep trying to coax
   the shriveled thing with your fingers. But no amount
of begging will lift that spiritless head. Squishing it
   into cunts and assholes is worse than useless.
Face it, it's time to elevate your appetite. It takes
   a sophisticated palate to stir an old cock to life.

XI, 66

You're an informant and a libeler,
a con artist and wheeler-dealer,
a dicklicking gladiator promoter.
Vacerra, how can you still be so poor?

XI, 87

You were rich, Charidemus, but started craving it
   in the ass. Women ceased to exist for you.
Now, you're working the widows. Ah, what poverty
   makes us do. It's even made a stud of you.

Sp. 35.

Da veniam subitis: non displicuisse meretur,
   festinat, Caesar, qui placuisse tibi.

Sp. 36.

Cedere maiori virtutis fama secunda est.
   illa gravis palma est, quom minor hostis habet.

Sp. 37.

Flavia gens, quantum tibi tertius abstulit heres!
   paene fuit tanti, non habuisse duos.

Sp. 35.

I hope you'll pardon my spontaneity: One shouldn't earn
  displeasure, by being in a hurry, Caesar, to please you.

Sp. 36.

To submit to power and survive is also to win.
  But the consolation prize weighs on the heart.

Sp. 37.

Flavian house, how much that third heir squandered!
  It would almost be better, to not have had the other two.

BOOK XII

Spring 102 onwards, in retirement at Bilbilis, Spain.

XII, 13

Genus, Aucte, lucri divites habent iram:
odisse quam donare vilius constat.

XII, 16

Addixti, Labiene, tres agellos;
emisti, Labiene, tres cinaedos:
pedicas, Labiene, tres agellos.

XII, 42

Barbatus rigido nupsit Callistratus Afro,
    hac qua lege viro nubere virgo solet.
praeluxere faces, velarunt flammea vultus,
    nec tua defuerunt verba, Talasse, tibi.
dos etiam dicta est. Nondum tibi, Roma, videtur
    hoc satis? expectas numquid ut et pariat?

XII, 13

The privileged, Auctus, rage and prosper.
Hate costs nothing, benevolence is expensive.

XII, 16

You offered, Labienus, three useless properties.
And got, Labienus, three silly queens. I see,
Labienus, you're still up the ass in property.

XII, 42

Bewhiskered Callistratus got married to rugged Afer.
    Legally, the way any maiden marries her man.
Torches shining on a veiled blushing face. Not
    a word of the old ritual omitted. Even the dowry
was formally set. But you're still hungering for more,
    Rome? You can hardly wait to see the babies?

XII, 55

Gratis qui dare vos iubet, puellae,
insulsissimus inprobissimusque est.
gratis ne date, basiate gratis.
hoc Aegle negat, hoc avara vendit.
sed vendat: bene basiare quantum est
hoc vendit quoque nec levi rapina:
aut libram petit illa Cosmiani,
aut binos quater a nova moneta,
ne sint basia muta, ne maligna,
ne clusis aditum neget labellis.
humane tamen hoc facit, sed unum,
gratis quae dare basium recusat
gratis lingere non recusat, Aegle.

XII, 59

Tantum dat tibi Roma basiorum
post annos modo quindecim reverso
quantum Lesbia non dedit Catullo.
te vicinia tota, te pilosus
hircoso premit osculo colonus:
hinc instat tibi textor, inde fullo,
hinc sutor modo pelle basiata,
hinc menti dominus periculosi,
hinc dexiocholus, inde lippus
fellatorque recensque cunnilingus,
iam tanti tibi non fuit redire.

XII, 55

Anyone who says you should give it away, girls,
is the stupidest absolute worst. I don't even kiss
for free, let alone screw. That's how Aegle
talks; and she gets a good price. It's sound
business. A nice kiss is valuable merchandise
she peddles at something close to larceny.
She angles for a pound of Cosmos' best scent.
Or four, even eight, freshly minted coins, just
so her kisses won't be stingy and spiteful, with
lips locked tight as a door. But beneath it all,
girls, beats a benevolent heart. Aegle, who would
never give a man her priceless tongue gratis,
never says no to a gratuitous lick.

XII, 59

When you return after fifteen years,
Rome greets you with all the kisses
Lesbia never gave Catullus. The whole
neighborhood descends on you: The farmer
with lips sprouting bristles hugs you like a bear.
Then the weaver grabs you, next the pissy fuller,
then the shoemaker who's just licked his cowhide,
then the proud owner of a sharp protruding chin,
then a cripple, and a runny-eye. And, here they
come – that cocksucker and cuntlapper, fresh from
their nap. Was this worth the long trip back?

(Martial was never away from Rome for "fifteen years". A dream, a Rip Van Winkle reverie in Bilbilis about the City he shared with his icon Carullus, a hundred years apart?)

XII, 65

Formosa Phyllis nocte cum mihi tota
se praestitisset omnibus modis largam,
et cogitarem mane quod darem munus,
utrumne Cosmi, Nicerotis an libram,
an Baeticarum pondus acre lanarum
an de moneta Caesaris decem flavos:
blandita quam sunt nuptiae columbarum,
rogare coepit Phyllis amphoruam vini.

XII, 73

Heredem tibi me, Catulle,
dicis non credo nisi legero, Cattule.

XII, 76

Amphora vigesis, modius datur aere quaterno,
    ebrius et crudus, nil habet agricola.

XII, 92

Saepe rogare soles qualis sim, Prisce, futurus
    si fiam locuples simque repente potens.
quemquam posse putas mores narrare futuro?
    dic mihi, si fias tu leo, qualis eris?

XII, 65

Lovely Phyllis stayed the night with me,
and gave herself generously in every way.
So I was pondering what gift might repay
such a lavish bedmate. A box of perfume from
Cosmos, something really nice from Nicerotis,
a full weight of golden Baetic fleece. Or ten
new yellow coins from Caesar's mint? But
then, snuggling up like a sweet mating dove,
Phyllis shyly asked for another jar of wine.

XII, 73

You tell me I'm your heir, Catullus. I won't
believe it until I've seen the ashes, Catullus.

XII, 76

An amphora goes for just twenty coppers, a peck of wheat,
    four. Drunk and bloated, the farmer goes broke.

XII, 92

You're always speculating, Priscus, about what
    could be, if we were suddenly the rich and powerful.
But can anyone really predict how he'd act? Tell me –
    if you turned into a lion, what would you be like?

THE EMPEROR AND HIS EMPIRE AT PLAY: SOME WAYS OF READING THE *LIBER SPECTACULORUM*

To the Ghost of Martial

Martial, thou gav'st far nobler epigrams
To thy DOMITIAN, than I can my JAMES :
But in my royal subject I pass thee,
Thou flatter'dst thine, mine cannot flatter'd be.

Ben Jonson

1. THE CONVENTIONAL ASSESSMENT

To begin with, there's the old dismissive view as summarized in the Encyclopedia Brittanica:

> Martial's first book, *On the Spectacles* (AD 80), contained 33 undistinguished epigrams celebrating the shows held in the Colosseum, an amphitheatre in the city begun by Vespasian and completed by Titus in 79; these poems are scarcely improved by their gross adulation of the latter emperor.

My 2nd edition *Oxford Classical Dictionary* similarly treats the *Liber Spectaculorum* as akin to juvenilia. "Its 33 surviving pieces record contests in the Arena without as yet full mastery of style." (I should note here that by the current numbering system, there are 36 poems in the sequence, plus a "questionable" 37th – about which, more later.)

But these are somewhat dated characterizations. The last few decades have seen increased scholarly interest in the sequence and recent commentators tend to gravitate to more favorable views. In his 2007 critique, *Martial, the World of the Epigram* the Cambridge classicist William Fitzgerald devotes a long chapter to the *Spectacles* poems and takes them quite seriously. But, he begins by noting one of the reasons the *Spectacles* are rarely translated (except in prose), and so remain among the least read of Martial's poems.

Standing at the head of Martial's oeuvre, the *Liber Spectaculorum* threatens to turn away the modern reader at the very threshold of his work. Even a sensibility dulled by contemporary screen violence may find some of it hard to take. For sheer physical repulsiveness, Spec. 9, in which a criminal is mauled to death by a bear is difficult to match. The cruel gloating at human suffering and the mockery of the tormented remind us of what has made the Roman Arena a source of such ambivalent fascination to Hollywood.

Fitzgerald does have a point. The carnage, both human and animal, of the Roman "Games" doesn't conform to what most might consider a fit subject for poetry. Especially when the depraved festivities are presided over by a (to us) repulsive "Caesar" who the poet appears to effusively apotheosize.

Even so, the upfront sexuality and salacious mockery that leads us to revel in Martial, made him unfit reading in Victorian times. Is there any reason why we can't also get past the gore? Especially when we consider that the sequence as a whole seems to have no prior model in Classical poetry and was written by an acknowledged master. If it fails, it's not through unoriginality.

I think the impediment for current enjoyment of the *Spectacles* poems isn't just their topic *per se*. Rather the subject matter combined with two interpretive issues. One, is the arbitrary dating of the work, with the presumption that the *Spectacles* are "the very threshold" of Martial's work. The other is the literal-mindedness of all too many scholars when they try to reduce the Roman epigram to prose.

To elucidate the latter, maybe it's helpful to revisit a Martial couplet addressed to "Catullus".

XII, 73

Hereden tibi me, Catulle, dicis.
non credam, nisi legero, Catulle.

You tell me you've named me your heir, Catullus.
I won't believe it, Catullus, until I've seen the ashes.

The surface interpretation is that the addressee isn't the poet Catullus, but some Martial-contemporary Catullus, a common enough name. The literal, obvious point is that the poem refers to the practice of falsely telling opportunists they're in your will, just so they'll do you favors. But why does Martial choose a name so important to him, his so often cited poetic model, and then repeat it? Yes, the poem says one mildly witty thing that literally stands on its own. But its epigrammatic resonance may just also infer a quiet homage beneath the surface quip. *How can I collect your poetic legacy, Catullus, when your poems are immortal?*

Neither I, nor anyone else, has any way of knowing what Martial's intent here was. But, I can offer the not all that esoteric thought that a poem begins when it imposes its own intent on the intent of the poet. Those who write poetry will recognize that faint sense of a hatched fish beginning to swim on its own. The poetry translator shouldn't have to choose between a narrow or richer interpretation, when the choice is really between taxidermy or gently freeing that anadromous fish in a new stream.

II. JUVENILIA, A CELEBRATION OR SOMETHING ELSE?

Kathleen Coleman is a Harvard classicist who has made a specialty of the workings of the Roman Arena. Apart from her serious academic work, she acted as a technical consultant for the script of Ridley Scott's film *Gladiator* (whose historical inaccuracies she subsequently criticized). She's also written on execution practices in the early Roman Imperial period – the time of Martial and the *Spectacles*. Particularly, what she terms "fatal charades", executions in which the condemned are made to play the roles of mythical figures for the entertainment of the Arena crowd. Only one (or possibly two) of the 36 poems in Martial's *Spectacle* sequence, portrays actual gladiatorial combat. But five recount execution entertainments.

Coleman has published a very helpful guide to the sequence, entitled *Martial: Liber Spectaculorum* (Oxford University Press 2006). She may have expended more time and research on the *Spectacles* than any current day scholar writing in English. The work is fertile ground for scholarly disputation because there are no extant contemporary or early references to the *Spectacles* sequence. Interpretations rest almost wholly on its sometimes arcane text. So, I think the first paragraph of Coleman's General Introduction, is particularly liberating to anyone attempting to translate these poems.

All that one can say with moderate certainty about this book of epigrams is that it comprises an untitled collection of uncertain length celebrating a series of unspecified occasions in honor of "Caesar" (unnamed); and it is attributed to Martial.

A browse of JSTOR, or similar academic paper troves, will produce scores of esoteric arguments attempting to tie the *Spectacles* to one date or another in the Arena, and to either the emperor Titus or Domitian. Coleman, who must have waded through seas of competing dissertations, finally concludes (although I simplify) that the anonymous Caesar of the *Spectacles* might possibly be Titus, but maybe more possibly, Domitian – or could just as well be both: a generic "Caesar", "an idealized abstraction". She also finds no compelling reason to presume the *Spectacles* depict only a single year's series of games, or that the work was presented to any emperor. And again, her well informed inconclusiveness allows us to imagine – just as Ridley Scott and scores of others have – an Arena that can only live now in our imaginations.

Coleman is just one scholar among many, and other qualified commentators may find good reasons to disagree with her assessment. But her acknowledgment of what we don't know seems especially important in an aesthetic context because it helps free a reader to interpret the sequence as something other than an adulatory bouquet of flattery written to garner an Imperial nod. We read (and translate) Martial for his sass, his realism, his refusal to hold much of anything sacred. The multi-dimensional, double and triple entendre of his epigrams is sui generis when he's at his best. And even the "opening of the Colosseum" dating makes Martial some 40 years old, hardly a juvenile. Acknowledging what we don't know allows a poetry translator to ask that essential interpretive question: *What makes this poem a poem?*

III: THE DIVINE CAESAR AND HIS ARENA

As the *Encyclopedia Britannica* notes , Martial's "gross adulation… of the emperor" is a major obstacle to our enjoyment of the *Spectacles*. But is this just a cultural obstacle, or maybe a matter of finding something lost in translation?

The *Spectacles* sequence is both unique among Martial's work, and uniquely Martial. His forte is his need and ability to make poetry from the distinctly unpoetic: deviant sex, money grubbing, bad language, the gritty underside of Roman life. The Arena seems a perfect venue for this. But unlike his other books in which various aspects of Martial as persona participate, both Coleman and Fitzgerald note that the *Spectacles* are more akin to a series of snapshots taken by an anonymous reporter. There is no distinct "I", just scenes and spectators.

For me, a twentieth-century comparison might be the short squibs that precede each story in Ernest Hemingway's *In Our Time*. Hemingway's news-clip subjects are similar to Martial's – violence, executions, gory bull fights. And like Hemingway, Martial's reportage does convey a marked enthusiasm for the animal fights. This is one reason I chose to break the sequence into segments preceding each "numbered book" of Epigrams. Another was to try to convey the purely subjective sense of incompletion and tentativeness I get from the work. As if the poems were still brooding on where they might be going.

Whether or not Martial's enthusiasm sincerely extends to the executions speaks to both the moral and aesthetic heart of how we read the sequence. And this question can't be separated from a judgement on the nature of the poems to the "divine" Caesar who's staging the executions. Are these poems simply panegyric, as a number of scholars, including Coleman, presume? Or sarcastic? Or – not untypical for Martial – epigrammatically both at once?

Can the glittering adoration of the games presiding Caesar, be read as a mirror held up to an emperor who's naked under his purple robes? Is something like that what Ben Jonson had in mind, writing to "The Ghost of Martial"? Jonson, who read his beloved Martial in Latin in a royalist age was, after all, not criticizing, but empathizing with him. Doesn't Jonson's ironic praise of James I by criticizing Domitian also infer Martial's implicit criticism? Isn't Jonson's epigram as much a comment on Martial the epigrammist as James the king?

Doesn't Martial's "animals haven't learned to lie" infer the question: What kind of lies do humans have to learn to be spared Caesar's mastiffs? Isn't the speaker's naked slavishness here, also, a kind of unembellished reportage? These questions, I think, can only be mulled in the context of the greater Martial canon and this is yet another reason to weave the sequence into the numbered books.

IV: Prometheus Crucified and Orpheus Gored

In the *Spectacle* sequence, we also have something truly unique in Roman poetry and even in Martial. The execution entertainments that Coleman dubs "fatal charades". A century before Martial, Horace famously observed *Graecia capta ferum cepit...* "captive Greece captivated her fierce conqueror...". While this was true for so many aspects of what we've come to call Greco-Roman culture, the opposite appears to have been the case with what might loosely be called spectator sports.

The "games" of the Roman arena had no counterpart in prior Greek culture. Armed gladiatorial combat was a Roman innovation. And trained gladiators, the most skilled of whom, in Martial's words, knew "how to win without killing", were only one arena attraction among many. *Naumachiae*, mock naval battles, were fought by war prisoners and convicts who were expected to kill each other off with only nominal survivors. There were similar butcheries of unskilled combatants forced to fight against gladiators or ferocious wild animals.

But even in the Arena, Greek myth and the Greco-Roman gods and demigods can be found. Toward the last half of the first century, A.D., probably beginning with Nero, the Romans began to develop a cruel innovation – execution entertainments in the form of mythological reenactments. These may have been only abstractly symbolic at first – as when, anecdotally, Nero had a miscreant burned to death with the *tunica molesta*, ("irksome shirt") – a pitch soaked tunic that turned the victim into a human torch – and dubbed him "Hercules" in memory of the fatal, poisonous "shirt of Nessus".

By the time of the Flavian Colosseum and Martial's *Book of the Spectacles*, these gruesome pantomimes took on aspects of sophisticated theater. The Roman *Colosseum* – much as our current day arenas – was a venue for gala presentations as well as sports. And in *Spectacles* 24, sophisticated, mechanized scenery, trained animals and an appropriately costumed "Orpheus" combine to portray the legend of the mythic prototype poet and semi-divine patron of the Orphic Mysteries.

But, what Martial describes is, at heart, a savage execution. The once sacred, imagery invoked as a backdrop for a sadistic practical joke as a grizzly-sized bear is released to tear the costumed victim to shreds. In the much later language of the U.S. Constitution, a "cruel and unusual punishment." In the last two of the three Mucius Scaevola poems in *Epigrams*, Martial recounts something similar: The reenactment of a secular myth sacred to the foundation of the Roman Republic with a ghastly hand incineration ritual. Trying to imagine anything equivalent in our civilization, evokes the unimaginable. The Philippine government taking advantage of Good Friday reenactments to actually crucify condemned criminals? A 19th century American public hanging in which the condemned is made to dress and play the part of Nathan Hale?

At this distance, 2,000 years later, the Arena's carnivorous appropriation of hallowed tradition conveys an eerie sense of cultural cannibalism. Of something slowly disintegrating at the heart of things. The first three *Spectacles* poems encapsulate a Rome at the pinnacles of both power and impossibility. A people, free now, to enjoy the pleasures of their former tyrant, Nero – whose pleasure was theatric cruelty.

Whose current *princeps* is proclaimed "father of his fatherland" in a Babel of foreign tongues. Is this just lame blatant flattery? Or an epigrammatic statement about a disparate people who can only be united with a mythos of the lowest common denominator - the Arena's pornographic cruelty?

Similar to Hemingway's squibs, Martial advances no conclusion, simply describes. And similar to Hemingway's aesthetic of "omission", one can find oneself pondering Quintillian's art of *emphasis*. A technique "…in which we wish to incite a certain suspicion without actually saying it. Not the opposite of what we want to say, as is the case of irony, but something hidden that is left to be discovered by the hearer…".

How might Martial's sophisticated circle – people like Pliny, Juvenal, Quintillian and maybe even Tacitus – read these execution poems? As celebrations of sadism, or as Hemingwayesque reportage that draws its emotional and moral weight from what's left unsaid because there's really no name for it?

Consider Spectacles 6, which deals with the forced, probably fatal, penetration of a woman victim, costumed as Pasiphae, by a bull the Arena's clever animal trainers coaxed to do the job. Not some low show. But rather, an edifying enactment for "Caesar" as the Arena presents him with yet another ancient wonder.

Iunctam Pasiphaen Dictaeo credite tauro:
vidimus, accepit fabula prisca fidem.
nec se miratur, Caesar, longaeva vetustas:
quidquid fama canit, praestat harena tibi.

That Pasiphae coupled with the Cretan bull – believe it!
We've seen it: the fable we used to have to take on faith.
You shouldn't be surprised, Caesar, at such an old tale retold.
Whatever myth sings, the arena presents you with.

I think the key phrase here is *fama canit* (fame sings). *Fama* is one of those all-purpose, multi-meaning Latin words, much broader than "fame" in current English usage. It can mean gossip, slander, idle chatter, myth or misinformation. Of the seven usages in the *Oxford Latin Dictionary*, "fame/renown/glory" is listed last. But doesn't coupling *fama* with *canit* (sings), seem to put a fame as glory spin on it? Yes, but the Pasiphae myth is about infamy not glory. A cautionary tale of a bestial human lust whose monstrous consequence – the Minotaur – has to be hidden deep in a dungeon labyrinth. The very opposite of "fame to sing about." So, at the least, *fama canit* seems sarcastic.

And let's stretch that a little further. Pasiphae is a myth, so "myth" is a valid word choice for *fama*. But who does the myth sing to? Is there an implicit double-entendre:? "Caesar… whatever myth sings (to you), the arena presents you with"? And is the double-entendre, only the resonance of a deeper, unmentionable that *fama canit* might bring to mind (if not to paper) in the context of this Imperial sex-snuff show. "Whatever's rumored to appeal to you, Caesar, the arena presents you with." Is this Quintillian *emphasis?* I've tried not to spin it one way or the other, but rather tried to retain the inherent harmonic polyvalence of Martial's Latin.

Conversely, in Spectacles 9, the poem whose cruelty so repulsed Fitzgerald, I consciously chose to emphasize a last line double-entendre in English that may be questionable in Latin. In that poem, Martial compares a crucified victim dressed as a stock mime-show character to Prometheus, the primordial benefactor of mankind – in some myths even humanity's creator. And, as in Martial's "Mucius" poems, no one really cares what the miscreant's done, what's important is the show… Does it matter?

He's certainly outdone the old storybook desperados. Their crimes are fables; his punishment, the real thing.

To deny that last double take is to deny our only path to the poem in English. I've similarly sought to avail opportunities to exploit double entendre throughout the sequence. To do otherwise, I think, would in itself be a spin that forecloses potential meanings.

V. A Questionable Ending: Spectacles 37

The text of Martial's *Spectacles* has come down to us in only a handful of manuscripts, all dating from well after his time. The current numbering of 36 poems combines these manuscripts and ends with two couplets that appear in only one 12th century source. Number 35 asks "Caesar's" indulgence for the writer's spontaneity as he hurries to please. Number 36 is one of those compact Latin statements that almost defies direct translation:

> *Cedere maiori virtutis fama secunda est.*
> *illa gravis palma est, quom minor hostis habet.*

Roughly:

> To yield to greater power and survive is also to win.
> But the consolation prize weighs on the heart.

In itself, a quizzical enough ending to the sequence. But a 17th century Dutch scholar's edition appended what would have been a concluding number 37, and this was included in many later editions. Sp. 37 is now generally excluded by modern scholarship, because it seems on its face incongruous. The prevailing theory is that the medieval "scholiast" who compiled its manuscript source interjected a later Martial couplet, written after Domitian's death. Given what Sp. 37 says, this may well be the case:

> Flavian house, how much your third heir squandered!
> It would almost be better, to not have had the other two.

Still, even if the dubious Sp. 37 represents only a misappropriated coda inserted by a medieval compiler – *it seems centuries ago someone else once read this sequence not all that differently than I am.* And, of course, once freed of the arbitrary "opening of the Colosseum" date, that line of "someones" could even extend to Martial. As I said, I often find myself thinking of the *Spectacles* sequence as notes for an unfinished work. Part sketchbook, part still unformed epic. A hesitant, Bulgakovian work for the desk drawer in Domitian's dangerous reign. If the *Spectacles* leave us with questions, perhaps they're also Martial's questions.

CPSIA information can be obtained
at www.ICGtesting.com
Printed in the USA
FSHW02n0504270918
52354FS

9 781848 616189